What happens when Christianity meets
men of other faiths—
or of no faith—
in today's world?

the listener

by H. S. Vigeveno

A Division of G/L Publications
Glendale, California U.S.A.

© Copyright 1971 by G/L Publications
All rights reserved
Printed in U.S.A.

Published by
Regal Books Division, G/L Publications
Glendale, California 91209, U.S.A.

Library of Congress Catalog Card No. 73-123872
ISBN 0-8307-0084-6

Contents

A teaching and discussion guide for use with this
book is available from your church supplier.

What's It All About?

If you are merely interested in gathering facts about other religions, then this is not the book for you. There is already enough literature available on what people believe and don't believe. This is not another volume in the religious spectrum.

But what takes place when men of different beliefs talk with each other? What takes place in such direct confrontation? Ideas do not meet each other in books or sermons. They can only explode in head-on encounters.

This book grew out of actual conversations with people who held a variety of views. Today's views. New ideas. Ideas of our time. *What they themselves said about their faith* forms the substance of this book. There is nothing secondhand here. I'm not recording what Christians said about non-Christians, but what a black leader affirms about the Black Muslims, a Spiritualist about Spiritualism and a humanist about humanism.

Here is what I did. After an initial contact with worthy representatives of other religions, I met them generally in their own surroundings, in an office, at

1

home, or we had lunch together. I talked with more than twenty people, individually. In each case I received permission to record our talks on tape. Large portions of this book are taken from the transcribed conversations, the actual phrasing and emphases of the people.

I did not run into anyone who was discourteous, cold or belligerent. Firm, yes. But always ready to enter into conversation and willing to share. I want to thank them for that. I was only turned down once. That man's views are obviously not included in this volume.

The people with whom I spoke remain anonymous. I have deliberately changed names, locations and personal details. They did not ask to remain anonymous. I made that decision to remain free in writing. For example, at times I have brought together more than one conversation in a chapter.

I do not mean to imply that I have obscured the truth, or colored conversations. I do not wish to falsely represent anyone. To the contrary. I have been most precise and completely honest. I have *deliberately* attempted to represent each individual fairly. I have bent over backwards to be realistic.

So, I am not reporting what *I think* people believe, or what I have read about their position. These are actual conversations. They happened, and I must add that I enjoyed them. Besides, I learned a great deal.

I hope you will find it as exciting as I did, to discover what happens when people who hold different views are not afraid to talk with each other—what happens when Christianity enters into conversations in today's world.

INTRODUCTION TO

THE REALIST

Fact is stranger than fiction

A realist is a person who looks at life from such a viewpoint that for him the language of religion is pure superstition. Or, at best, the figment of one's imagination. The realist looks askance at the man of faith and thinks that he ought to grow up from all that is supernatural, or just get with it in the modern world.

When the realist weighs the world of experience against the realm of faith, the seen against the unseen, he comes to the conclusion that what he can feel, touch, hear, smell and see is for real.

In this group of realists I have placed the following three: a scientist who is an outspoken atheist, a humanist who has no interest in the supernatural, and a businessman who believes on Sundays but can't put it into practice the rest of the week.

A strange grouping? Perhaps.

The scientist represents all modern men who trust in man's technological achievements, in his great conquests of space, time, the elements and life itself. He measures and calculates, and that is his total picture.

The humanist happens to be by profession a Unitarian minister, who has thrown out the window all the beliefs he once held. He sticks to ethical relationships, social pressures, action groups and man's ability to achieve his own ends.

The businessman is not a total unbeliever. However, he cannot entertain any of his beliefs as he immerses his active mind into the greedy world of the dollar. He represents the many who can't harmonize religion and business. He, too, is a realist who denies the relevancy of faith.

No, not all scientists are atheists, nor are all Unitarians humanists. All businessmen do not divorce business and religion. Yet in these three we encounter very outspoken realists who look at their world scientifically, economically and with essentially **human** eyes.

CHAPTER 1

The Atheist

Through a mutual friend we had made the appointment over the phone. I drove to the beautiful campus where he is an authority in his field, and after parking my car, walked over to the brand-new science building. It towered over the campus, and from one of the top floors I caught a view of the city.

The professor led me into his busy office. His desk was full of papers and books. The shelves behind him were filled. He held a stubby cigar with his teeth and a welcoming smile with his lips. He didn't look like the typical professor with hair all askew. His was neatly trimmed and combed. Nor did he look like the absent-minded scientist with bushy eyebrows. He was completely in control of his activities and expressed his thoughts precisely. His mind moved like the precision tools with which he worked in physics.

He was British and charming. He gave me the early impression that he thoroughly enjoyed life.

I introduced myself and told my purpose. He responded eagerly. He was not in the least bit hesitant about stating his views. We discovered at once that we were moving in different directions. It would become increasingly difficult to find common ground. He made this painfully clear as he launched right in: "I come from a fairly well-established family of atheists," he began. "My grandfather was a leading anticleric, my father was a good old-fashioned rationalist, and I absorbed all this as a small child. What you are taught when you are young builds into you such a strong prejudice that any other point of view seems completely irrational."

He leaned back and looked straight at me a moment. Then he went on: "So for me, anyone who believes in God, believes in an absurdity. I think primitive man went through a stage of intellectual development. He saw external phenomena and attributed those to spirits or gods, but to me that's just a primitive belief. It has no right in the modern world. You see, I'm coming clean at the start."

"You've given me a lot to go on already," I said. "But you don't mean to tell me that all scientists are atheists, do you?"

"Not at all. I know some very intelligent people who hold the opposite point of view, who do believe in God. There is a wide variation of different human beings in any field. And I will be frank to tell you that I have a son in his late twenties who is a most devout Christian. He and his wife carry their religion to excess. So, in my case, it's not like father, like son."

He smiled boyishly and seemed to relax a bit more. So I asked whether he had discussions with them.

"Oh, sure," he replied. "We have long talks on the basis of morality. And this is where we disagree. He thinks God makes a difference concerning morality, and I don't. You don't have to believe in God to be moral, do you? But, anyway, I'm a scientist and my whole preoccupation is with things rather than people."

"Has your pursuit in science influenced your thinking even more? I mean, has it confirmed your early atheistic teaching?"

"Very profoundly. The fact that I'm an atheist is the result of my upbringing, and I'm a scientist because of my natural tastes. As I said, I'm more interested in *things* than in *people*. That's putting it extremely crudely, but I've always wanted to know what makes things work. What really drives me on is the discovery of harmony in the physical world. You might say that my entire preoccupation is to find out *how* things happen."

"But I receive from you even in so short a conversation as this, a great feeling for people. I can't fully accept your statement that you prefer things," I said.

"Well, my interest in people came as a later development," he replied. "At first it was things. I was withdrawn as a child and teen-ager. I participated in sports, but all that was not the really interesting thing to devote my mind to. Only after marriage and having children did I discover how important people are. Perhaps I should say that my statement about things versus people was a gross oversimplification."

He smiled again and puffed on his cigar as he leaned back comfortably in his swivel chair. There was nothing odd about him. He certainly did not fit the charac-

terization of a science professor. He was very human.
His feelings ran deep.

"Now, in trying to discover *how* things happen,"
I wanted to pursue his comments, "to what extent can
you dismiss from your mind *why* they happen? That
is, the ultimate question?"

"Well, there you are leading straight into a misconception. These are not questions. They are nonquestions."

"What do you mean—a nonquestion?"

"Something which has the form of a question in
words, but behind it there is really nothing. There is
no question at all. You say, 'What is the purpose of
existence?' Now, I've just put a question in your
mouth. . . ."

"Fine. Let's take it."

"It implies that there should be a purpose. That's
already begging the question, for there *is* no purpose!
Things have *happened*. But they haven't happened
purposefully." Every word was heavily emphasized.

"Not for a reason?"

"I would say not."

"How do you know?"

"I don't. How do you know there *is* purpose?" There
was a short pause. Since I didn't answer, he went on:
"It is really an unsatisfactory emotional attitude to
look for a purpose. Your question is therefore not a
question at all."

"Doesn't it bother you, then, to find the meaning
of your existence?" I changed the word "purpose" to
"meaning" deliberately.

"Well, now, a lot of modern philosophy is concerned
with the analysis of meaning."

"Do you as a scientist pursue this question of meaning?"

He nodded affirmatively.

"I raise the question because I was talking with an engineering student who said he was so busy with all his academic pursuits that he had no time for any other reading," I explained. "He eliminated all philosophy, literature and religion while he narrowed himself down to science."

"Two comments here," he said, puffing out some smoke. "Students in our universities are so hard-driven to get their degrees that they are forced into specialization. Secondly, engineers tend to be among the least imaginative. In fact, I don't call engineers 'scientists.' But the faculty here in physics is widely interested beyond the required professional reading. I keep up, to a certain extent, on the literature and thinking of our generation."

"Do you read such atheists as Bertrand Russell and Jean-Paul Sartre?"

"Certainly, although Sartre nauseates me. He asks too many nonquestions about the individual."

"Have you also read those who write from a Christian perspective, such as T. S. Eliot and C. S. Lewis?"

"Yes. Eliot writes beautifully, but he has no direct appeal to me. That's probably because he writes as a Christian. I find C. S. Lewis an obscurantist who believes in ghosts and devils and all that nonsense."

"Have you read the theology of Tillich or Barth?"

"No. When it comes to that kind of professional theology, I can't understand how they can be serious about it. I feel an enormous gulf between them and me."

11

"But, of course, they pursue the questions of 'why' and 'who' with the same seriousness and devotion which you give to the question 'how.'" Having made my point, I switched abruptly: "And, as you said earlier, you hold to certain moral behavior."

"Certainly. This is where my son and I conflict. He thinks he has a basis for holding moral principles, and I don't. Although I hold the same views. I have no belief in God."

"*Why* should you hold these views then?"

He stopped a moment to think about it. I could tell, however, that it was not a new area for him.

"This is a very interesting question. Essentially I think a cultural tradition, a *Christian* tradition, has rubbed off on me. I have to be honest about this. I behave in a certain way and believe in certain things that are good to do without any reason. And I couldn't really argue with someone else who behaved differently. My son said that you should behave because God wants you to."

Then he added, off the cuff, but most pointedly: "He has an easy way out. . . ."

"For you it is more difficult then, since you have no reasons for your ethics. And yet you hold to a set of values."

"Exactly. Besides, I would say from my observation that the people who are thinkingly critical of Christianity are on the whole more moral. Most conforming Christians don't think very much of the implications of their faith."

I couldn't argue his point and told him so. Although he had given an unequal comparison—a thinking realist and a conforming, sheeplike Christian. He should at least have compared an ethical atheist with a concerned Christian. And so I raised a related moral question: "What do you do with the question of guilt?"

"Explain what you mean by guilt."

"Take it from a psychological point of view. A person sees a psychiatrist or minister out of a sense of guilt."

"Guilt for something specific or general?"

"Perhaps specific. Although guilt is, after all, a universal phenomenon. Most human beings feel some sense of shame, some sense of failure."

"Well, I often feel a sense of failure," he said quickly, drawing on his pipe. "There are many things which I have left undone which I should have done, or done better. Of course I feel guilty. Not enough to see a psychiatrist though." He smiled at his subtle humor. "But the remedy ought to be in me. I ought to be able to look at this squarely. I can't put my troubles on someone else. I suppose that is a very arrogant attitude."

"Let's say you don't feel any responsibility toward God."

"Exactly. The responsibility of guilt is toward myself. And if I have let other people down—which also gives me a severe case of guilt—I try to put things right."

He paused again. Then he added: "I thought perhaps you were thinking of the guilt of Adam and Eve, of original sin."

"No, not *their* guilt," I said. "Yours and mine. But since you mention Adam and Eve, let's get to the beginning of things. What is creation to you, if there is a creation? As a scientist you surely ask such questions?"

13

"That's part of my professional work of course. Origin of the universe and what happened a long time ago is to me a profound matter."

"Is there an origin, a beginning?"

"Philosophically, no. It's always been there. It will always be there. We can't go back and check!" Out came that contagious smile with a good-humored chuckle. "As a cosmologist I'm keenly interested in the big bang theory. By this I mean to say that matter started and then burst apart quite suddenly—with a big bang. We live in the continued expansion of that explosion. Many hold to that theory, but it doesn't appeal to me."

"And so?"

"And so I hold to a steady stage development. I like the theory of continuous creation, the theory in which new matter is appearing continually in the universe. "But," he added, "I must admit that the evidence is rather against this."

"You would *like to* believe it, but you can't in all honesty?"

"One has to keep an open mind, and the picture changes constantly. Even in the last ten years! As a professional physicist this is where I get my sense of awe. It's such a tremendous universe. Human beings are stacked on such a small planet in such a small system of a vast universe. . . ." He smiled, and for a moment seemed lost in the wonder of it.

I hated to disturb his mood: "This sense of awe. . . ."

"It's a matter of psychology. It's not developed in all people, but I think it's one of the most powerful factors in making people, eh, religious."

"So you have this sense of awe, but if you will allow

me to say it, you refuse to let it guide you beyond scientific limits. You are fenced in by evolutionary theories. You dare not climb over this fence to faith. That would be off limits, scientifically speaking."

"Well, if you like. You see, there's *nothing*. Because anything that would make this jump to create the world would violate the harmony it already has."

"Creation by God sounds like a miracle to you?"

"Yes."

"And any miracle is to you a violation of that harmony?"

"Oh yes. A very ugly thing. Esthetically and intellectually repulsive."

"Even a miracle of healing?"

"Yes."

"Things should keep to their normal course?"

"The normal course is complex enough without intervention."

"Sir, do you mind if I take this question of miracle to the greatest miracle of all? We Christians affirm, as you know, that God became man in Jesus. What is your evaluation of Jesus?"

"Frankly He puzzles me. He existed historically. I find that easy enough to believe. But His teaching does not always sound practical. It doesn't seem to be worked out in the world. They are hard sayings, hard to live out."

"I have to agree with that, although I think His words must be properly understood. And they haven't always been."

He understood what I was driving at, so he continued: "Well, I think Jesus was an ordinary person. He had extraordinary insight well ahead of His time,

15

but I don't think it's very useful to the modern world."

"What do you make of the fact that He thought Himself—and said Himself to be—equal with God?"

There was a long, painful pause. He had wrestled with the question before, but he now framed his reply carefully: "I don't know whether He meant that literally. I would suspect He led His disciples to think that He did. But I think He meant it allegorically. Now, you see, I don't think this is a very important question! Christians think so, but to me it's not even interesting."

He was trying to drop it, but I couldn't let him off the hook just like that.

"Is it *not* interesting to you that here appeared a man in history who said He was equal with God? That He represented God? That anyone who saw Him had looked upon the Creator of the universe? Suppose this actually took place? I'm stating a supposition. Doesn't that concern you at all?"

"No. It's obviously wrong. It presupposes there is a God. That's nonsense in the first place. And then, if there is a God, this isn't the sort of thing a God would do. If people want to believe it, all right. But it's primitive. It's not even worth thinking about."

"Why do you reject the question?"

"Because, as I say, there is nothing there. Nothing to answer. Why am I here? I'm here as a result of natural processes. That's all."

"Do you think the world will grow up to the point where primitive superstition, all this religion will vanish?"

"I used to be optimistic and hope it would take place in a hundred years. Now I think it will take a thousand to two thousand. Yes. It will happen."

"A thousand years from now. . . . What of the future? Your future? Is there anything beyond death?"

"No."

"Then, what is the purpose of my life here?"

"There is no purpose."

"When you consider your children, do you want their lives to continue?"

"What do you mean by *want?*"

"Suppose one of your children is suddenly killed in a tragic accident. . . ."

"Do you want me to believe that somewhere else there is another existence? I can't. There can be things which are great misfortunes."

"Do you think this is fair?"

"That's a question for a believer in God! But if you don't believe, you don't ask it. You know, I could be very critical of a God who allows this kind of accident or tragedy to happen."

I was still working on the same point: "What of this great mind you have given years to develop? Now, suddenly, it's all over!"

His answer was blunt, quick and pointed: "Sad, isn't it?"

"Yes," I said slowly. "Why develop it then? Why all this effort?"

"Oh, well, I think that's by no means a good question. It would be the most unsatisfactory thing *not* to develop it! It gives me great pleasure to make the best of my life. Isn't that the purpose of your existence also?"

He let this sink in and then admitted: "I must be honest. You touch on certain issues which are difficult

17

for a person of my persuasion to answer. Where does this all come from? This system of values, these concepts of right and wrong, this need to explore, this desire to develop oneself? Still, to me, that's a slanted way of asking the question. I can't even consider them. In the end there are *only* scientific questions!"

We were interrupted and he was called away to a meeting. As we walked out of his office together he told me he had enjoyed the conversation. I felt that he had. He lit another cigar and stepped into the elevator.

When he hurried off to his meeting, it looked as if he'd already forgotten our talk. It had been so foreign to his academic pursuits. And yet I couldn't help but wonder as I returned to my car whether some of the questions on meaning and morals had perhaps penetrated his airtight, scientific frame of reference.

Only *God* knows.

CHAPTER 2
The Humanist

The Unitarian Church dated from the early days of the city. It was practically downtown on a busy street, big and old. A cobblestone entrance led to a large but cold office in which three secretaries moved about. One with a pile of papers in her arms immediately turned and explained that the minister was out for a few moments. He would return for our appointment soon.

She wore no makeup, dark horn-rimmed glasses, and a loose sweater which was two sizes too big. An older woman sat quietly, evidently waiting for the phone to ring, while the third never looked up from the mimeograph. I entered the large, cold room to wait for the senior minister.

Ten minutes later he entered with youthful step and energetic manner; a large, virile man surely in his sixties, growing a sizable mustache. He gave some orders to his staff, shook my hand vigorously and invited me to climb the winding, stone stairs up to his office.

19

He had lots of life in him, and when he began to talk, I could sense at once that he was a preacher *par excellence,* a man who knew how to capture a congregation as he was about to captivate me with his forceful manner. His mind proved to be as sharp as a razor.

"I have been in the Unitarian Church since the thirties," he began after he'd settled down. "Before that I was a Methodist minister, although I was raised a Quaker. I actually became a Unitarian when I went to Boston University to teach. But I had been moving in the direction of a more scientific approach to religion for some years. I also married a Unitarian girl, and I'm happy in this contemporary, yet historic, group. Over the more than thirty years I have been in Unitarianism, I've seen it change."

"In what way?"

"When I became a Unitarian, we were overwhelmingly theistic. Liberal of course, but most of us believed in God. The humanists, who disregarded the supernatural, were a minority among us. Every year there was some resolution in our assembly to have them read out of the church. Today, without question, the majority of our clergy are humanists. Our young people are not concerned with the question of God. We are involved in many areas of religion in life, but not in the philosophical arguments about the concept of God. We have no creed, no statements of faith. The great majority of our people do not think in terms of a personal God."

"In what sense then do you call yourself a *church?*" I asked.

"We are a church because we are a religious society.

We use the word 'society' more than we do 'church.'
It's a hang-up for many, especially our Jewish friends."
He sat there relaxed behind his neat desk in his beautifully paneled study. His library looked orderly and imposing.

"Are there many Jews who become Unitarians?"

"Not as many as some think. About twelve percent. That's about the same number as ex-Roman Catholics. But half of our people are come-outers from nowhere."

"How large is Unitarianism today?"

"We are a small sect, if you will. Only about a quarter of a million people. But Unitarians are historically important in American life, in literature, in politics. We have a high batting average in the professions and public affairs. We are often dissenters and get the spotlight in the media, out of all proportion to our numbers."

"Is Unitarianism dwindling then?"

"No, it is growing. Not only in universities, but also among the working classes. And actually our influence stretches far beyond our membership. For example, we have more educators in our movement than any other vocation! And, of course, there are many concerned humanists who think as we do, but who are not Unitarians."

I wanted still to pursue this idea of the church, because I was suddenly beginning to realize that this humanism had very little to do with worship. Nor did this religious humanist differ much from the atheistic scientist whom I had interviewd only a couple of days before.

"You meet together on Sundays and hold a *worship* service?" I asked.

21

"Let me correct you. We have a service on Sundays, yes. It's not a worship service. It's the celebration of life. We have our own songs. We give pulpit editorials, readings and addresses. But no prayers. No hymns to God. We are not addressing or singing to the Deity. It is an hour of fellowship, of discipline, of social expression, of dedication in humanistic terms."

"I still can't seem to mesh the words 'humanistic' and 'religious.' How does this humanism differ from any social organization or ethical society?"

"Your question reflects a provincialism about the meaning of religion," he said at once. "Religion is not necessarily theistic. Some great Asian religions, including Buddhism, do not believe in God. Religion is a cohesive force for man's inner relationships with himself and his universe. Past, present and future. It has to do with his goals, his values, his social action. When I go to Japan, for instance, to talk with educated Buddhists, I find a commonality of objectives which astounds me."

"Do you feel a kinship to all religious expressions?"

"That's right. Our vocabularies and rituals may differ, but we are doing the same things."

"I notice this universality in your pictures." I was nodding toward his paintings and etchings around the office. "I recognize the picture of Gandhi."

"That's a rabbi," he said pointing to one of the black and white drawings. "This is Mark Twain behind you. Over here an ordinary worker, symbol of the masses doing pretty shabby jobs until we can help them. You recognize Paul Robeson, a personal friend. And Gandhi, of course."

"But not Jesus?"

22

"No. I have yet to find something which would represent to me authentically what He is."

"What of a Rembrandt? I'm not suggesting an original, of course."

"Jesus is not omitted by intention," he sighed. "The historic artists were either by conditioning or by the contracts they signed, very much in a rut. I also found when I came here, a cross on an altar. I moved it away because it represented nothing to some of the freethinkers and Jews who were coming. However, I bring Jesus into my sermons more than most. I taught Bible, you know, at the university. One of my gripes is that we do not train our ministers in the New Testament."

"What is taught at seminaries?"

"Church administration and counseling, of course. Philosophy, ethics, social science. Our men are well educated, but they have tremendous gaps in church history and doctrine."

"And the Bible?"

"Well, remember that I don't accept the Bible as inspired any more than the religious books of other faiths or Emerson or Huxley. Inspired words are still being written and spoken today. But I do consider it necessary for study *historically*."

"And Jesus?"

"Historically, too. Jesus was a prophet, a teacher, the suffering servant. He was a member of the early resistance, a pacifist, possibly an anarchist and a man very skeptical of institutionalism. And, as I said, I refer to Him from time to time."

Later I read five sermons which he had selected for me as definitive of his beliefs. In these five sermons

I found one reference to Jesus, except for the specific paragraph in answer to the question, "What do Unitarians believe about Jesus?" And that reference said that Jesus was in error to believe the Kingdom of God would come in some dramatic way.

My host was very relaxed, and yet he talked with an intensity undimmed by the years. He leaned forward most of the time, looked straight at me and without any hesitation expressed himself. The question of God was not a question that concerned him in the slightest. I could not get him to talk much about God.

"I do not find any necessity or occasion for ascribing personality in this sacredness of life, no necessity to assume a first cause or a final destiny," he stated in one of his sermons. "If you have found God unnecessary in your life, so be it. But let us be certain that if the idea of God dies, man does not die with Him. The goal is man alive, growing, master of himself and the world around him."

I probed a little further: "As to Jesus' claims to be the Son of God—do you dismiss these?"

"Who am I to dismiss them? I take them as historical claims, although I do not accept the Bible as an authoritative description of what either the prophets or Jesus actually said. As to Jesus' sonship, it isn't relevant in today's world. I wrestled with this as a Methodist, but when I left the Methodists, I simply left those problems behind."

I wanted to pitch one other question about Jesus to this man who had left his Christian upbringing. He may have considered it a hard-breaking curve: "What about the resurrection of Jesus?"

He kept his bat on his shoulder momentarily before

24

taking a slow, half swing: "Eh, well, I can't remember any time in my life when this was a question of importance. I was taught a way of living. There were no rewards or punishments, except in the present world. In my early days I found that my congregations didn't expect me to preach doctrines with force. They wanted me to get on with the business of the church. And in the Unitarian church there were no doctrines expected. I could get right to the business of involvement."

I came in with a fast ball: "But that wasn't actually my question. What do you make of the resurrection of Jesus, *historically?* How do you explain the beginnings of Christianity apart from the resurrection? As you know, it was central to the preaching of the apostles."

"I would say certainly that these men believed. But what led them to that belief, I don't know. What phenomena occurred, if they did, I'm not prepared to say. I think we'd better have an open mind to the origins of Christianity. There will be a lot of surprises coming forth from recent discoveries. As for me, I'm a freethinking humanist who does not expect another life. I do not give assurances of life after death to my people either."

This led to a discussion about the Universalists who had united with the Unitarians. They used to teach that all men will be saved, that there is no damnation and hell. He said that this was early Universalism, but it isn't an issue any longer. Just as Unitarians once placed the emphasis on one God instead of the Trinity, but have outgrown that issue, the Universalists don't bother to discuss the next life. Both approach the twentieth century with sweeping, relevant, active humanism.

"The real teaching of Jesus is that all men are good and have the potential of goodness in their hearts," he advised me. "Therefore no man is damned forever. So, our emphasis is on the worth of human life."

"All men are good?"

"Rather than all corrupt in original sin."

"How do you square this with the world around you?"

"That's a very good question," he laughed. "The problem is far more complex. Why does man do the dreadful things he does? Well, there are conditioning factors which make us act as we do. Once you understand this, you become optimistic about man, what he can do, what he wants to do. Man responds well when he is surrounded by love—like children. And man has enormous drives to become responsible, happy, generous. I have an increasing confidence that we won't blow ourselves off the planet."

"Even in the face of nuclear . . . ?"

"Even in the face of the nuclear potential," he anticipated me. "We've had it since Hiroshima, and we're the only ones who have used it. And it has backfired on us."

He had entered his field now. He felt at home, having disposed of the questions concerning Jesus and moved into the area of social concern.

"Look, I'll sum it up this way," he said. "Where the old religions made the supreme object God, the new make it humanity. The great question has been, 'Where will you spend eternity?' The great question now is, 'Where and how will you spend the rest of your life?' I don't believe in a Creator. I've been brainwashed by the scientists. We are in a natural universe in which we either make it or we don't."

"I've been thinking of one of Jesus' parables," I told him. "I'd like to see what it means to you. It's the one about the farmers who have leased their land. The landowner sends his servants for a share of the product, and the farmers not only ignore them but kill some of the servants. When the owner sends his son, they get rid of him also. As you know, Jesus was talking about Himself as 'the son of the owner who gets crucified.' Doesn't this story have anything to say to you about God and the Son of God and man in God's world?"

"That's a fine parable. But I'd preach a sermon on the destruction of natural resources by 'us farmers.' We forget the people who will come after us. Greed and selfishness rule us and we misuse the resources whether they come from God, nature or what-have-you. That's the point. . . ."

He drifted away from the story, but such a free use of Scripture completely obliterated the meaning of Jesus' words. He had a point in our abuse of nature, but that was surely not the primary intention of the parable!

"This is an old question," I said as I tried another approach. "You are a moral person. You hold a system of ethics. Why? To what extent can you embrace it without relating it to God?"

His answer was immediate and pointed: "I do not use an authoritarian morality of any kind. Man makes his ethics out of what is good for him and his neighbor. There are no absolutes. There is no finality. Only situational ethics. And I think that we'll get better behavior out of people and less guilt without impossible standards."

"Are you saying that if you remove the authority (whatever it is) you will lessen man's guilt?"

"Exactly."

"What if you remove the authority and guilt remains?"

"Then you haven't accomplished it, have you? It hasn't worked."

"That's my point. *Why* hasn't it worked?"

"Because the social taboos are still there," he said.

"Would you accept that the concept of *God* may still be there? Because we've been created by Him?"

"No, because I don't believe in God." There it was again. Firm. Definite. Final. "I would say that our concepts of right and wrong are part of our tribal inheritance, passed on from generation to generation. We are conditioned by many things, and they play a bigger factor than the books on theology would indicate."

"No God-given consciousness?"

"No." But then he let down a little. He made an admission: "I don't profess to know where all our insights come from."

"You were brought up as a Quaker, you told me. Do you ever think of the 'inner light' any more?"

"Yes, it's a concern to me. Even though I'm a humanist. We should not treat lightly the insights which come from—we don't know where or how. The scientist may experience it and he acts on it. So the hour of silence for Quakers is a pretty good hour to let whatever operates on the subconscious operate, whether

28

it's natural or supernatural. I'm not terribly interested in what it is. I'm just interested in the product. A new way of relating to your neighbor. Or to yourself. Or to your world."

Whether Unitarians would still be around in another century, he wondered. There was not that much difference between them and any intellectual, ethical or social action group. In a way he didn't care, he added, and when I asked him to sum up what he was essentially saying to the world, he concluded: "I guess what I'm saying is that everyone of us must *do what he must do*. That's what I tell my people. Don't feel guilty if you can't do what others are doing, but do what you must do. Be yourself. Follow your conscience. Do what you must do *at your depths*."

We stood up and said good-bye. He ushered me out of his office and jokingly told his secretary that he'd told me all he knew.

I couldn't help but recall as I walked past the secretary with the horn-rimmed glasses that a rabbi had once commented that the Jews had been playing this game of activism far longer than the Christians. "When the clergy become more worldly," he had commented, "the world goes to hell all the faster."

The main business of the church is, after all, about life and death, God and man, time and eternity.

CHAPTER 3
The Businessman

On the top floor of the swank bank building I looked through his windows at the magnificent view all around, a view of the mountains under the blue sky which was just beginning to smog up. Down below, the traffic was ever winding itself around the freeways, as an occasional beep or siren rippled its way up into that exalted office.

It was air-conditioned and cool as I sat comfortably in an armchair, waiting for the executive to get off the phone. He was placed perhaps six inches higher than I behind a formidable desk, which appeared like a fortress. He held the high ground up there, looking down on any customer about to storm his stronghold, while he won the battles.

I glanced about the tidy office at the picture of his blond wife, an air shot of his mammoth factory, a snapshot of his yacht and a sculpture of Durer's praying hands. The last looked a bit out of place.

His efficient personal secretary breezed in periodically to toss a note on his desk or remind him of a coming appointment. "She's a machine," he commented. "Very efficient." She was smartly dressed in a pale blue and white tailored suit with blue and white shoes to match. He replaced the phone on the multibuttoned receptacle and came straight to the point: "What do you want to talk about?"

"About business and ethics," I said.

"The one thing you'll get out of this," he started, leaning back with his hands clasped behind his neck, "is that in business there's a great deal of inconsistency. On the one side you'll find the rough, tough, hard-boiled businessman, and on the other a fairly decent human being. But not too often. Because the name of the game is *profit*. Protect the profit. Generate the profit. And if you don't, they get somebody who does."

"The profit motive runs the business world?"

"Sure. Shareholders sit down at the annual meeting and say, 'Hey, the dividend isn't quite as good as it was.' So you've got to produce."

"*How* you get the profit doesn't matter?"

"Well, yes and no. You must get it in a legal fashion, of course. But you'd better get it—or else." His hand was slicing through the air as though he were chopping wood. "Now, we are very fussy about the inventory tax, but I know very few who are this fussy. When you take inventory for yourself and it comes to a tax, you all of a sudden become a very bad counter. The objective is always to make as much money as you can."

"So you operate on this principle?"

"Yes. Look. In every corporation there's usually a driving force. When a small company becomes big,

31

it's as a result of one man. And that man's whole philosophy, his whole way of operating, is to drive the organization."

This very night he had to talk to the chief in New York. They talk long-distance every week.

"I haven't had any snotty letters this week from him," he commented. "So I know I'm in for it tonight. And I'll lay odds of twenty to one that I'll be given a bad time next week. That's the way he operates. His method is to work you over *so* hard that you're *so* shook, you'll drive, drive, *drive* . . . to accomplish what he wants accomplished!"

"You mean to tell me most businesses . . ."

"There has to be a driver. Somewhere. He checks everything. And I, in turn, drive my salespeople. I give them the devil. They have to produce. We're paying them enough to! And even your own people don't care about the corporation. Nobody does. They've got a job and that's that. As long as they get theirs, they're happy. The name of the game is profit."

With all this talk he'd opened the door to the subject of our discussion. "Some of these businessmen," I started, "are surely religious. They have some religious upbringing, and . . . ."

He leaned forward immediately, anticipating my question. "To be as candid as can be, I think religion and business have no connection," he said flatly. "I just got off the phone to a man in trouble. He wanted a thousand shares of some stock in exchange for his part. I offered him seven hundred and fifty. He had little bargaining power, and I knew it. I took advantage of him. He was in a spot he couldn't get out of."

He stopped a moment and then went on fervently:

32

"Now it wouldn't be a bad thought to say that since I gave this bird this deal, he's not going to be in a good position to kick me around either. See, I won't have to give him even this much in the future! My mind automatically runs this way, and I say to myself, I can pick up a good deal here. So I jump."

There was a long pause. We both let these ideas settle for a moment. In spite of his philosophy of business, he told me he was basically religious. His parents were conservative politically and religiously. He had high regard for his Sunday School teacher and the ethical teaching of his pastor in that sleepy Midwestern town. But now he looked straight at me and said with great force: *I think business would just shock the daylights out of you!* It is the most greedy, political, power-drunk . . . well, it's a constant maneuvering for advantage. The greed motive. And you play this game like a skilled gambler. It gets to be like breathing."

"What about the human factor?"

"You don't weigh the human factor at all. If you do, you're a dead duck."

His secretary hustled in with some money. She laid it on his desk. He picked it up and started to count it.

"You don't even trust your secretary to cash your checks for you," he said as he stuffed the money in his wallet. "You count it. You check everything, and you find out the very first time you don't, you get had. Somebody is always after you. Just as bad as you're after him. The customer wants to get the most for his. By any means. He doesn't care what he does to you."

33

"But I'm sure there are plenty of businessmen who go to church."

"Sure."

"But how does this fit? What you're saying. . . ."

"What has church to do with it?" he broke in. "You go to church, sing hymns, say your prayers, enjoy the choir and a sermon. You get something to think about."

He paused a moment.

"Take this example about a supposedly religious man I heard about," he continued. "He sells five watermelons for a dollar. So people stop to buy five, and he gives them six. They call it to his attention and he says, 'I know it.' They ask him why. He says, 'I like to be a good fellow.' Now, we all like to be considered good fellows. But this farmer isn't such a nice guy. He's a *crook!* If he were legitimate, he'd put up six watermelons for a dollar, but he puts up five, gives you six, so you can praise him. He's greedy. He wants to be praised!"

"A kind of reverse crook."

"Exactly. It all comes back to greed. The older I get, the more I've thought about it. The greed motive seems to be dominant in all human beings."

"But what of the person who doesn't push like this?"

"He's a jerk." He answered without emotion. "He gets nothing accomplished. There's a fellow in our San Francisco office. I worked him over this morning till he's bleeding. The only way I can get him off his tail to do something is to get him so upset that maybe he'll get moving and do it. He's the nicest guy in town."

"Talking about nice guys, what's your comment on the Good Samaritan? Suppose a businessman goes to church and hears that example from the pulpit?"

"This can happen. And when the preacher gets to you on Sunday, you become a better driver. You're less discourteous. You become a little more thoughtful of others, of the little fellow who hasn't got brains enough to keep up with you. You may even go out and do something fairly nice for somebody."

"You try to keep a good face forward?"

"You never know when your factory might burn down, and you may need somebody to come in and help. You should have some good relationship someplace."

"Now suppose a man has made his pile." I was still questioning this greed motive. "He's satisfied his greed motive. He's got everything. What about him?"

He stared out of his window a few seconds, leaning back in his chair.

"I'm thinking of a man like that. He's old. He's made it. So why in the world doesn't he sit back and enjoy it? He probably thinks he's indispensable. He works himself sixteen hours a day. Why? As near as I can figure it, he gets satisfaction out of showing you that he's fourteen times smarter than you'll ever be."

He stopped a moment.

"On the other hand," he continued, "families expect more. A friend of mine bought his daughter a good little used car. She's managing to have more things go wrong with it, because she didn't want a good little used Thunderbird. She wanted a brand-new little Thunderbird. She's going to repair him into a brand new one. Nineteen years old. See?"

"I understand," I said. "But what about loving your neighbor as yourself? Does the average businessman apply this? Or does he just forget about it?"

35

"I think he just forgets about it . . . just forgets about it," he repeated under his breath. "Because the minute he'd make that kind of a move, he'd be scalped. He doesn't think the golden rule, and if he does, it won't last over fifteen minutes. But here's where the inconsistencies come in. We like to do things for people, like that farmer with his watermelons. We kept a man on the payroll for nine months, even though company policy dictated no more than five weeks. He's back from his illness now and not producing. But he's old. Fifty-eight. So what are you going to do? Fire him? Where can he get a job? And old Mr. Tough in New York knows we aren't getting our money's worth. But we cover him."

"How many companies would do this?"

"Not too many. But don't get the idea we're such good guys. Look. I don't think religion gets to the average man. If it does, he's out of business. Oh, I know dozens who'll tell you they've built their business by the golden rule, but I don't believe it. They drive hard. They're hustlers. I had lunch with this religious man, this *very* religious man, and he told me plain to my face—if he had to do business by the golden rule, he'd be sunk. Just plain sunk. And he's very devout!"

Even though he talked with me in this way, I knew that he had personally taken time with people who were going under. He had offered genuine help. And now he was very conscious of the greed motive which he saw within himself. It may be true, as T. S. Eliot has said, that avarice will prove to be the great vice of the twentieth century.

We talked a little about Abraham and Jacob, both

of whom were rich businessmen. And Jacob used some devious means to make money. But with this background I now asked him about those praying hands by Durer. He smiled.

"Yes, I've had a few comments on it. The old man in New York says he knows why they're here: I should get on my knees right now. As for me, I just happen to like them. They say a lot."

"It's a different note in this efficient office. Everything else speaks of, well, business."

"Yes, nobody likes a losing ball team. But the hands, I just think they're great."

"I'm coming to my real question," I said and he nodded assent. "You have surely heard that Jesus said you can't serve God and materialism. You can't serve two masters."

"I'm sure you can't," he said quietly. "And I'm sure many men give something to help the church. It's a completely separate project. Their good guy image is coming forward. But as they drive home from the church meeting, they may be planning what they'll do next to whom."

"Then are they serving God really?"

"Well, at one point. Not completely, of course. You see, I don't look at any of us as being completely good. So the service God gets (except perhaps from the very few) is pretty minor. He gets some, but not much. We're in the ball game for ourselves. There's no other way of looking at it, if you want to be realistic."

Then he asked me candidly: "Do you think I'm bitter?"

I just threw it back: "What do you think?"

"No, I don't," he answered. "I'm just being honest.

I'm greedy automatically. I don't even have to work at it. That's the way man is."

"What you're really saying is Christian." I couldn't help but interject it at this point. "Christianity doesn't say man is good and doesn't need a thing. Christianity says that man is greedy and selfish. This is why Christ has come for our salvation."

"Does God really expect us to serve Him completely? I don't think so. If I were to run my business asking, 'Is it right that I do this to that man?' I couldn't do it. I'd ruin my business. I can't worry about every person I deal with."

"But would you run him into the ground?"

"Not necessarily. I'd just give the gravy to the best advantage moneywise. You are successful or you fail, based on how good your judgment is."

"You've really been saying two things," I said.

"That's the inconsistencies I told you about." He shifted. "We've got a soft heart but a tough hide. Look. If I wanted to be completely successful, I'd tolerate none of this keeping a man on the payroll who can't produce. If you really want to serve that old god money, you don't get soft. Have I confused you enough?"

In a way he had. God and greed. Not black or white. Nothing simple.

"When I think of morals and principles, it gets to be a highly individualistic sort of thing. You can't generalize," he went on. "I've developed a healthy respect for some people. One man I know is so nice and quiet and neat and you think this guy couldn't harm you if he tried. But he's the shrewdest toughy I ever met with the morals of a snake. One Sunday morning he called up a competitor, another manufacturer, because he wanted to merge companies. Sunday morning at seven-thirty, mind you.

"His competitor sat up in bed and asked him whether he knew what day it was. He had a calendar, said this man. Did he know it was Sunday? Yes, so what? That it was *Easter* Sunday? His competitor told him he was going to Sunday School and church as was his custom, and he'd talk about it Monday. This bird couldn't wait. He never called back."

He was leaning back again. Although he seemed relaxed, his active mind was racing a hundred miles an hour.

"I'm a realist. I have to be. I have to keep my head above water in this mad game. But, you know the question you should be asking businessmen to get some very interesting answers?"

He pricked my curiosity, and I waited for his own suggestion.

"What do you think is going to happen when you die? Well, the answer you'd get from the men I know who are outstanding and really at the top is always the same. These crack executives will put it in one word—*nothing!*"

"You really think so?"

"No question. Now—that's all that matters. I don't happen to believe that, but it will explain a lot of things. Why we're in this rough, merciless, competitive world. A lot."

I finally asked him: "If you were a minister and had to preach to businessmen, what would you say?"

"Have you ever preached on greed? I think you couldn't preach on it too often."

We finished talking now, since his secretary rushed in with another note and he was anxious to make his next appointment. He was in this mad whirl for profit, but his childhood values would not leave him completely alone. The question would be, which master would control him, which would win in the end?

To be realistic about it, we have only *one* heart to give in allegiance—to God or material things. So, what difference does faith in God make for a hard-nosed businessman? And what, after all, will set him apart from the practical humanist or the moral atheist?

SUMMARY

The Realist

So here they are. The scientist, the humanist and the businessman. How can we penetrate their realism with the good news?

The businessman may be the easiest after all. If he listens to the church from time to time, perhaps what he will hear about materialism will begin to disturb him. He may be forced to face his greed. And maybe since he doesn't believe in life after death, by attending church on Easter he may have to encounter the fact of the Resurrection. That could change his entire perspective.

The humanist may be more difficult. Since he rejects the supernatural, it is on the human level alone

41

that Christians can reach him. Why does he help humanity? Why is he a humanitarian? For which reasons does he want a better world? From where does this desire originate? Such questions can't be logically dismissed. They will ultimately wind their way back through faith and hope to God.

The scientist may become disillusioned. Many have. They face realistically the disastrous prospects of a nuclear age. Here may lie our hope. Since Jesus has not come for those who are well but those who are in need, only out of disillusionment will man turn to the light.

These are realists. But Christianity is very realistic.

Although it is impossible to please God apart from faith, the good news is founded on solid facts. Facts, such as the resurrection of Jesus, will attract the realist. They are worthy of investigation. I, for one, could never be content unless I held to a logical faith. When Jesus said we were to love God not only with our soul but with our whole **mind,** I think He meant it.

INTRODUCTION TO

THE ESCAPIST

Oh that I had wings like a dove
to fly away and be at rest!
PSALM 55:6

The escapist looks at life and religion completely opposite to the realist. If the realist considers only the scientific and factual, the escapist leaves the world behind and flies off into the blue. He runs away from reality and seeks something bizarre, new, and probably insupportable.

I have chosen three examples of such escapism.

The first is the rebel. Often he is young, but he need not be a teenager. Yesterday he was a beatnik, today he is known as a hippie and tomorrow he will have a new name. This nonconformist, antisocial, and antireligionist escapes from the world of reality into his own system or nonsystem.

45

The second is the faddist. Currently he is a devotee of Transcendental Meditation. Formerly he was interested in yoga, Vedanta or Zen. (He may still be, of course.) Tomorrow he will follow something else that's new, riding the current craze for all it's worth. I talked with two very knowledgeable people who teach Transcendental Meditation.

The third is a spiritualist who generally finds life too painful to face and death too harsh. I spoke with a medium who well represents the occult. Her escape is into the spirit world and conversations with the dead.

So the escapees in religion are diametrically opposed to the realists who have their own hang-ups. Yet the essence of the Christian faith keeps on eluding those who run away from the truth.

CHAPTER 4

The Rebel

At this writing he is known as a hippie. Formerly he was a beatnik. Tomorrow his name will change, but he will still be a reactionary. Army psychiatrists admit that yearly over a hundred thousand soldiers bring their behavioral problems into the military. They call them marginal soldiers.

The young people who run away from home, drop out of school and make their way to some rebellion centers in New York, San Francisco or a host of other places, are frequently of some church background, and some may even be ministers' children. One of the problems I encountered in talking with these rebels was explained to me by a minister who works in their midst. Many are drifters, on the run, here today and gone tomorrow. They do not attend scheduled meetings. They have no leader or spokesman.

But there are also adults who run away from a society

that threatens to make conformists of them. I made contact with a man of unusual talents and incisive insight, who has shown a decided interest in the rebellious young adult. A lecturer by invitation at universities, he has been able to sit down with them in their own surroundings, although he himself was not one of them. His hair was neat and trim, and he wore no beard or ragged clothing. His life seemed to me even overly managed, and his business establishment where we met was the very essence of cleanliness and order.

The only touch that did not fit his properly ordered life was the green sport shirt he wore with a brown tie and a nondescript but colorful sport coat. He expressed himself in perfect English and delved right into his subject.

"I became involved with the hippies through a friend. But I did not only meet with the kids who had run away from home. I spoke with people who had held very good jobs and were the product of a good education. One I remember is a qualified architect. He works just enough to keep himself going. Another is a writer. Another a landscape gardener. These adults have become disenchanted with society, and especially with war and segregation. They have reacted because they've seen too much and too little."

"Do you want to explain that?" I asked as we sat at a table in his gourmet restaurant.

"They've seen too much of their society and its limitations and tasted too much of their own rebellious attitudes. But they've seen too little of the nature of their reaction, why they've dropped out or run away. So, their problem is not society out there, but freeing

48

themselves from all the frustrations, all the wild patterns, all the reactions within. They supposedly examine the cause of their pain and misery, but that makes them open. Most people in our society when you approach them, say with religion, feel they are being attacked. The rebel seemingly has nothing to lose. He's dropped out not only from school, but culture, society, religion—everything!"

"Have these people actually forsaken all this?"

"Theoretically," he said. He held his chin in his hand and pondered the question a moment. "I would say they have forsaken it physically. But psychologically they still have a social consciousness. For example, they identify themselves with each other. Like with like. They have formed a tight, conventional, rejective society anywhere they congregate. They reject all the time. They fear society."

"So they have left their families then?"

"Yes. Not only young people who have left homes and parents. But fathers, even mothers, who have forsaken their children, people who have rejected responsibility. They have turned their backs on the world of order, whether it's the order of clothing, of exchanging goods at the market, or of relationships."

"But how do they make it financially?"

"They work and make enough to tide them over. They maintain themselves on the minimum."

"What about insurance policies?"

I knew the question was ridiculous, and sure enough he laughed.

"No, of course not. They have nothing to look forward to." At once he became philosophic again. "They seem to think they are living in the moment. It is

49

an insidious illusion, you know. By saying the words 'I'm living in the moment,' I'm not necessarily living in the moment. It's not so easy. You don't leave the past and you still head into the future."

"Don't they consider themselves free?" I asked.

"They consider themselves free," he said. "But freedom is not freedom when I have rejected something. Freedom is the absence of rejection. Freedom is being freed of all my reactions. Besides, I should add that a number of these people are running away from the law. They are wanted for support. Government agencies can't find them. They may be on a drug rap, or they've absconded from taking care of their families. Some even have a morals charge against them. So they are not *free.*"

"How widespread is it?"

"I don't know. I won't make accusations. But I have talked to more than a few who fit these categories."

"Do they admit to the morals charges?"

"Oh, yes. They admit it as long as they know they will not be reported. Most of them still use drugs. Very few have seen through the danger of the habit. Periodically when they get into a bad mood and a problem presents itself which cannot be resolved, they resort to drugs again. They are very lonely, often frightened people unless they're with their own kind."

"Do you know any who did not revert back to drugs?"

"No," he said and moved around a bit as he expressed himself. He enjoyed this kind of analysis of the situation. "They may lay off for a while, but they return, particularly when a problem arises which they can't handle."

"Why has the guitar become a symbol for this community?"

He took a deep breath.

"Well! When I'm bored and lonely, and there's nothing happening inside me, it's amazing how a good rhythmic beat will fill that emptiness. People run away from the noisy city, but they can't take that inner silence. So the beat goes on. Let me tell you about one person. She was a very capable, intelligent private secretary to an executive. She fled the whole thing. But even in her self-exile, she is terribly lonely. When she is overcome, tears are her only answer."

He now talked about the uniqueness of this movement, although the rebellious, adolescent approach to life has always been in the world. Some experts predict, however, that the present actions will not be a mere fad, but will offer frustrated individuals an escape. He leaned an elbow on the table: "This is one of the first departures in this present culture. Years ago people rejected. But they didn't reject in concert. They didn't form groups. They had no publicity. They did not create a voice which said that things aren't right. And so what do we have? A new community with moral freedom and little sexual pressure. A boy and girl live together until they separate, and that's that. It isn't like the executive who keeps on changing partners. Not at all. It's a bit more honest. They live together as though married, but no one knows for how long. They are free to do as they want."

"What if there are children? Who assumes the responsibility?" My question naturally followed.

"Well, there is some responsibility. And a few of the adults are becoming concerned about education.

51

How can they send their children to the public schools, when they can't accept society's ways of education? I think they may develop their own schools, without pressure, without grades, without comparisons, in a free atmosphere."

"And when it comes to that point, you don't think the rebellion will die?"

"Some of the older ones are becoming disillusioned. It's getting a little thin and wearisome, because the early rebellion is always exciting. After it wears on, unless there's a *new* rebellion, it wears off. The dramatic is lost."

"And then, I suppose, those who ran away will come home again to assume the role of the ordinary citizen."

"Not necessarily," he said and his voice rose in pitch. "And did I tell you that the ones I contacted were vegetarians? Not for health reasons, but because of the cruelty involved—to animals."

"Cruelty to animals?" The words sounded strange to me. "You told me many had left their families; some even their children. What kind of cruelty is that? Isn't that a far greater cruelty?"

He agreed. "This is what I meant when I said they have seen too much and too little. It may be too painful for them to look into this. The whole inner mechanism which rejects must be looked into. Not the thing we reject, but *why* we reject it!"

"One other thing. You said that these people use drugs. Haven't people in all cultures always used drugs? What's so different about this?"

"I was a musician years ago and I knew many who took drugs. But they were not rejecting society. They wanted more of it. They wanted to get their kicks, you know. More money. Bigger positions. More success. But these young people rebel against materialistic promises because they do not make people happy. They weren't happy in their affluent homes. So, drugs have come to them at a time of stress and pain. They have been a panacea. They don't own cars or television sets, so drugs offer an escape."

"Have they sought anything else?"

"Yes. Astrology. Fortune-telling. Witchcraft. The occult. They're open to everything. And all of this forms a wonderful distraction when you have nothing to do. Those who haven't made it in this world want to make it in the next! They investigate all sorts of things."

"And you don't worry about food because it's always going to be there?" It was a leading question.

Again he became almost philosophic in his reply: "I'm not so sure about that. There is worry. There is anxiety. You see, even though you reject the outer world, the *inner* world still remains very much with you."

I grunted. He went on all fired up.

"In fact they have all the same problems in their community. All their emotional, social and sexual relationships are filled with tension. Just because you leave society behind you, you don't solve your problems."

"What about a fear of death?"

"Sure. Everyone has a fear of death. You don't run away from it by rejecting society."

"Is there any belief in eternal life? Any such hope?"

"When people are interested in living now, they don't think about tomorrow."

The conventional Christian approach would not

53

penetrate the escapist state of mind. I followed another direction.

"Why the dirt?" I asked.

"I think cleanliness is synonymous with order. They reject the whole package. Like Hell's Angels with their black leather jackets. It's the same thing."

"I just thought of something," I interjected. "At the other end of society we have the bums. They're dirty, too. They're down and out. They've rejected and been rejected. . . ."

"I see some comparisons," he replied quickly. "The dirt. The rejection. They help one another. They run away from responsibility. They have escaped into alcohol, the others into drugs. Perhaps the comparison ends there. You see, these so-called hippies in these funny little places have some beautiful art objects. Can you imagine a bum on skid row with art objects?"

He had a point. I now attempted to become specific again: "Most of these people have not only grown up in Western society, but also in a Christian environment. Have they rejected all this also?"

"Yes. All religions. They examined the Hebrew-Christian culture, and they have seen all of it end up in continual war and bloodshed. So, what does it all mean? To them, the only 'Christian' who lived, died two thousand years ago."

"They accept Jesus?"

"I won't say that, exactly. They point out that no one has truly followed Jesus. At least the people they know. They don't want to join anything. They don't want to listen to anyone who will tell them what they have to be or do. There's a song: 'Don't change me, don't rearrange me.' You might say that's the escapist

54

pattern and the church can't reach them. They've rejected all of it."

"Do they desire to return to the original teaching of Jesus?"

"No, not at all. They are not interested in examining the words of Jesus. Let me put it this way. They can read Bibles all over. They don't want anyone to tell them what it means."

"Do they actually read the Bible?"

"I doubt it," he said as he stood up. Other duties were pressing upon him and he had to attend to them.

I thanked him for his time and insight into these reactionary patterns.

So, in many cases the doors are closed, just as they are in certain countries to the missionary. Certainly the conventional, organized church is shut out. Some do reach the young in small groups, but it's slowgoing. And often the church back home balks at such unorthodox methods.

It may seem that those who reject everything have thrown out the baby with the bath water, but the activity of God is ever strange and incomprehensible. He is at work even in the rebel who has run away from home into the far country.

CHAPTER 5

The Faddist

He stepped from his Lincoln Continental motor car, the picture of health. He sported a glowing tan and was immaculately groomed. He looked much younger than he was. And when he smiled generously, extending his hand in welcome, the monograms on his shirt swam into view, framed by shiny cuff links.

She was in her forties, trying to look much younger. She wore an original creation in white, a peekaboo dress with a high neck. Her bleached hair was up on her head in Marie Antoinette style, and she held it like a queen. A huge emerald flashed on one hand, while her long nails were manicured in silver. She was very chic.

We met at a restaurant in the early afternoon, and they ordered their breakfast. Phil and Georgia were devotees of a Hindu teacher, whose present following is over a million in fifty countries. The Maharishi

Mahesh Yogi, commonly known in India as "His Holiness," was partly a representative of Hindu thought for Western man and yet he offered an entirely new approach, they told me.

"He is not teaching a philosophy at all," said Phil, who had studied for three years. "The only requirement is abstinence from all drugs before you can learn the technique. Whatever you are, stay that, he says. And you'll be better. If you're a Catholic, you'll be a better Catholic. If you're a Christian, you'll be better. If you're Jewish. . . . You see, the whole world is doing the same thing anyway."

"Doing the same thing?"

"Yes. We are all seeking the true identity, the true self, the absolute, God, whatever you want to call it."

"The name doesn't matter?"

"No. It is the source of all things, the transcendental. We need a technique to become conscious of that."

"What if a person is an atheist?"

"That's beautiful," chimed in Georgia. "They're the best people in the world."

"The skeptics go in innocently," said Phil. "And our technique must be approached in all innocence. Like a child. The nature of meditation is to flow to its source, which is pure bliss consciousness. But when the mind thinks of something, the mind is held there. Like a dam. And the river can't flow to the ocean."

"Hmm, hmm," I grunted.

"The use of meditation allows the mind to flow freely, removing the dams we set up in our thinking," added Georgia. "Nothing is strained. We do not concentrate on anything. It's not contemplation. It's not mood-making. It's not emotion. There may be some ritual from Hindu tradition, but it's not the important thing. The important thing is the individual who meditates. . . ."

"You see," broke in Phil, "our whole approach is one of education. It's scientific. It's not strictly a religion. The consciousness expands. Neither study nor preparation are required to obtain results. It is completely free from hypnotism or spiritualism."

"You accept all religious expressions of all people?" I asked.

"Yes."

"That's Hindu philosophy," I emphasized. "All inclusivism. Christianity is in a way of speaking exclusive. It makes a particular claim to a particular revelation."

"A person asked the Maharishi one night whether he believed in something particular," answered Georgia. "He said, 'I believe in everything.' Everything! Meaning, that in everything there is truth. When you enter a room, you turn on a switch. The light goes on. This is what we're doing in meditation. It isn't a matter of faith or believing this or that."

"What about reincarnation?"

Phil came back into the conversation now.

"He believes in it personally. But he does not get into it one way or the other. It has nothing to do with philosophy."

"Are you interested in reincarnation?" asked Georgia.

"Well, you spoke of oneness with God, the river flowing into the ocean. I want to know what happens if you don't achieve it in this life?"

"We probably won't," she said.

"We can't do it in eighty years," added Phil. "I

may not know where I am, but I know I'm not there yet."

"So you will have to live again on earth?"

"I don't know, but my personal opinion is that I would have to."

"Then you do not believe in Christian salvation here and now, but in an endless process of many lives with causes and effects," I said flatly.

The waitress came to serve their breakfast. She ate scrambled eggs with toast, and he cut into a juicy steak with eggs. Since I had lunched, I joined them with a cup of coffee.

"What is really the essence of your movement?" I asked.

"Our meditation. We meditate twice a day," answered Georgia. "A half hour each time."

"On what?"

"On that word which is given us by the master. We dismiss our conscious thoughts and follow that word. This is how we transcend."

"You do not use any scriptures then?"

"No. That would be thought again. Meditation is the only technique in the world today where a layman can transcend the entire relative field twice a day."

"During my encounters with other religions," I told them while taking a drink of coffee, "I interviewed a Zen Buddhist priest and meditated in his temple. We sat with our faces to the wall for half an hour in silence. Then we stretched and did a little ritual, walking around the room, and sat down again cross-legged to meditate. What's different in your teaching from Zen?"

"Whatever you think on when it comes into your

mind is concentration, not meditation," said Phil. "If I sit and meditate on love, I cannot transcend because I hold my mind at that level."

"But we sat facing the wall. There was nothing."

"You're not getting the point," he countered, swallowing a piece of steak. "There is no technique. There is no vehicle. It's hard to explain. Nothing captures our mind. We don't do anything!"

I felt as if I was being spun around, blindfolded. There was a technique, but when it came right down to it, there wasn't any. What was the point?

Georgia tried to clear up my obvious confusion. "You are part of the whole," she said. "You are part of God as the stem is a part of the flower. But what is it after all? Sap. Just sap. So, the closer you get to the source of everything, the more you improve."

As she talked it was clear that here were parallels to the teaching of Ernest Holmes, who had founded the *Science of Mind* magazine and the Religious Science movement. The magazine enjoyed a circulation of over one hundred thousand, while the Church of Religious Science was a happy, conforming and thoroughly relaxing way of enjoying life.

Suddenly Phil made me sit up. He began to tell his personal story. Before he was thirty he had been a professional gambler. Then he was soundly converted to Christ.

"Mine was a real conversion, and I knew it," he said.

He didn't become just an average Christian. He became a convinced, outspoken, witnessing Christian, who felt it his duty to tell everyone about Christ lest they should wind up in hell. He led his own parents to Christ, and being an ordained evangelist, baptized them.

I could tell from his persuasive manner that he had been extremely capable as an evangelist. He sold himself. He had the polish of the most able salesman.

"I spent seventeen years in several countries on the platform. I preached to thousands. I knew all the leading evangelists and I had my own association. I saw thousands of people accept Christ. No one can ever take that from me. That was an important step in my life. It gave me a reason for living. And," he added for my benefit, "anyone who is engaged in that work now, is doing a great job. They are bringing thousands of people a step up in understanding."

"And then what happened?"

"Then I reached a point where I could no longer say, this is all of it. For me personally there was more than I was telling. But Christians weren't ready for it."

"Then you think that you have advanced *beyond* Christianity?"

"I wouldn't say advanced," he said. "But for me there is more. I now appreciate Jesus even more because I know what He is really saying."

Although he was divorced during this time, he said, that was not the factor which drove him away from Christianity.

"The road has not been easy. There's a lot of pain in growing. But now I read more subtle meaning into the Bible. I see Christ in *all* people, not only Christians."

"What do you really think of Jesus now?"

"He is a great teacher. He is from the Godhead.

I believe Jesus to be exactly what I believed before, only I believe more about Him."

"Is He the *only* Son of God?"

"No. There are others. The only reason why you and I aren't, is because we haven't evolved to that understanding."

"But you are surely aware that this is a Hindu concept, that there are many teachers who have come into the world from God. The Scriptures speak of the Messiah, the one Saviour for the world."

"Christ hasn't changed. I have," he replied.

"Is He the Judge of all men?"

"He is that each day of your life. Now."

"A great Christian leader who lives in India puts it this way: 'When Buddha died, he went to Christ. There was nowhere else to go.' "

"Exactly. Everyone must go to Christ. But we get Christ mixed up with Jesus. You see, the Christ-spirit lives within me, just as the Christ-spirit lived in Jesus."

I couldn't help interjecting: "You know, I asked a person in Religious Science that same question and he also said that the Christ-spirit was in Jesus. The Christ-consciousness. And he said that everyone can become like Jesus. Everyone is a son of God. We only have to recognize it."

"I agree with that view," said Georgia.

"It's not what the Bible teaches, is it Phil?" He looked at me for a moment but didn't say anything. I went on: "Take such a text as John 14:6: 'I am the way; I am the truth and I am the life; no one comes to the Father except by me.' What do you do with that?"

"All right. No man comes to the Father but by the

way Jesus did it. That's the only way you can do it."

"But 'by me' means the person of Christ."

"Yes, but He represented a spirit. Don't you remember how He said that we could blaspheme Him, but not the Holy Spirit? That means Christ put Himself lower than the spirit. The spirit is the true revelation of the "absolute." Not the body of Jesus."

"What about the *body* of Jesus? What about the resurrection?"

"Beautiful! He had to show people that if a man dies, he will live again. People weren't sure of that."

"Was this a bodily resurrection?"

"Look," he said, not really facing the question, "this is not so special. People have bodied and reembodied at will. Many gods have come to earth."

Again his interpretation was broadly Eastern rather than biblical.

"Do you mind a personal question?" He nodded in the affirmative. "What happened to your thinking? Why did you leave Christianity, when you once believed it so completely?"

"Frankly," he said as he leaned forward, "I ran into too many questions for which I had no answers. I always had to revert to the providence of God. Someone would ask me why a child was born crippled and another blind. Well—the providence of God. Why were men not born equal? Again, the will of God. But God is no respecter of persons. Logic, love, and because I believe God is a God of order led me into Transcendental Meditation. I found no other explanations."

"Then you left because of the question of suffering?"

"No, not that. That was only one reason. I reached a point where the logic I learned from the Scriptures and life led me beyond Christianity."

He brightened up considerably and faced me with that same fervor he had exhibited in his evangelistic meetings: "Man is to know *everything*. There is nothing that we are not to know. And we must know everything before we can become God again."

"Christianity is really a very exclusive thing," said Georgia in a rather cutting way.

"Yes, it is," I agreed. "Not exclusive in the sense that it says everybody is damned who is not a Christian, although some have preached that, too. But exclusive in that it speaks of the one Saviour for all the world, one incarnation, one atonement, one resurrection, one mission."

"There isn't anything in the Bible that's not true," she now added demurely. "But it's the manner in which you interpret it. It needs to be properly understood as leading toward. . . ."

"You see," cut in Phil, "Jesus was the greatest teacher of karma, of cause and effect. What you sow you reap."

"Aren't you again interpreting the words of Jesus through Hinduism?"

"I'm interpreting," it was a quick and pointed correction, "I'm interpreting the words of Jesus in a *universal* scope."

"But the problem with that is, Phil, that the Bible presents a particular people, who were chosen of God to bring the Redeemer into the world. I grant you, this is a problem. The question is, why did God choose the Jews?"

"But let's get back to the premise," he said. "You're starting in the middle of the story."

"I'm beginning with Abraham."

64

"God chose that people in that land at that time to bring enlightenment. But that same God chose other men in other parts of the world as well, to do the same thing. Long before Abraham."

It was a most peculiar interpretation. I was positive that Phil was not acquainted with the scriptures of other religions, for they did not teach what he had said. No redemptive task for the world. No mission.

"Where Jesus said that He was the door, it must not be interpreted as the only door," said Phil as he put the cap on it. "It must be understood as the door *principle*. We have misunderstood Jesus."

"Have we misunderstood His suffering on the cross?"

"He didn't suffer. The Christ-spirit was God. God cannot suffer."

Georgia was anxious to finish our talk. She turned to me and said sweetly: "We think you're doing a great work. Every minister is. We're happy with what everyone is doing as the world evolves. It's wonderful. The world is so beautiful. What you're doing is beautiful. You're bringing light."

"We're all growing. We're perfecting. We're maturing." They chimed in together, sharing these positive ideas. "It's beautiful. It's wonderful. And the more that come along, the happier our trip is. If everybody in our country will meditate, we will have peace for a thousand years. It's just beautiful."

I couldn't help but notice that in the background a piano had started to play some soft, dreamy and escapist music. It all seemed to harmonize perfectly with our conversation, as we left the restaurant in a friendly manner to go (what proved to be) our separate ways.

65

CHAPTER 6
The Spiritualist

She was a medium. She transmitted messages. She received her information from "cosmic forces." She was a part of that ancient practice which can be traced to Assyria, Babylon and Egypt and was once known as witchcraft; a tradition of those who communicate with unearthly spirits.

In the Victorian era spiritism was a big thing. Sitters clasped hands around tables that wouldn't hold still. Blaring trumpets flitted above their heads. Visions were conjured up in the dark, and voices spoke in an eerie chatter.

Today mediums are hard to find. They're not listed in the yellow pages. There is no central agency of referrals. There are, however, groups, societies, and churches which belong in this movement and practice occultism. But occultism covers a wide range of all that is hidden, obscure and hypnotic—including fortune-telling, clairvoyance and astrology. Some advertise.

That's how I found her. I had managed to lay my hands on a couple of publications in this field. One informed me that some four to eight million persons in the United States are interested in metaphysics, new-age thought, prophecy, psychic research, mental and physical health through natural methods, healings and parapsychology. Articles included horoscopes, flying saucers and communication with the dead. Ads from all over the world purported to tell your future, your fortune, give counseling, healing, teach e.s.p. (extra sensory perception), read hands, cards, stars, handwriting and even lip prints. She ran her ad also.

She was ordained by the Universal Church of the Master, after she had attended classes taught by a qualified teacher. She had mastered the basic principles of spiritism, but each student takes a different amount of time. Some may never make it. She had the title of "reverend."

Her home was converted into a church. She lived in the rear with her husband, and she had fixed up an area with folding chairs facing an altar of flowers. Some traditional pictures of Jesus were also on display. There was a record player and soft organ music.

She had been psychic since childhood. She had been in spiritualism for about five years. Her unusual powers enabled her to foretell events. So she had felt a desire to be trained for this work, she told me as we sat in the back of her church.

"There are quite a good number of spiritual organizations in most countries," she informed me in a soft

• and pleasing voice. She was a dark and attractive middle-aged woman, charming in her manner and quite willing to share her beliefs.

"Some of the spiritualists have seances. We do not. We do not turn the lights out. Our services are held just as in any church."

"Would you say you are another form of Christianity?"

"We are definitely Christians. Our teaching is quite similar. Some of our churches, for example, are called 'The Temple of the Holy Trinity,' 'The Church of the Spirit,' and ours 'The Church of Light.' "

"You weren't always a spiritualist, were you?"

"No. Only a few years. I was brought up in several protestant churches, but I have gone *beyond* this to really try and help people. To give them messages. So in our services after prayer and a few hymns, the people write out a question, and I give them messages."

"Where do you get these messages?"

"The spirit forces tell me what I am to say to people. These forces are the helpers of Christ. Now anyone can become a helper of Christ, anyone who has left this earth. You see, we think of earth as this plane, and those who are dead on a higher plane. Any of the so-called dead can be one of these spirit forces."

I tried to have her feel more at ease with me, and so I asked whether she did any private counseling.

"Yes," she said. "People come to me with their problems, and I try, with the help of these forces, to bring them comfort, renewed faith, courage, and a better outlook on life."

"Then you consider yourself a medium?"

"Oh, yes, I do," she said pleasantly. "But by medium

I mean that I'm the connection between two worlds. The cosmic forces cannot always reach the living whom they want to help. Not everyone can tune them in. So, we as mediums bring forth the words of these forces."

"You do understand, don't you, that the word 'medium' is usually used in a derogatory way?"

"Yes," she said. "But I never try to give out bad or shocking news. Some do this, of course, but I can't. I want to help people and not try to scare them."

I persisted: "But what happens in the event you are given some bad news?"

"I won't tell."

"Do you think of these cosmic forces as good or evil?"

"There are evil forces," she answered almost immediately. She was expressing herself firmly, but quietly. "We surround ourselves with the Christ-light. Then nothing else can have power over us. Some people claim to be possessed by the evil forces, but evil forces seek darkness. That is why we never turn the lights out. We seem in this way to get closer to the light and to God."

"Tell me how you think of God."

"I don't think of God as a personality. Not as He. God is 'it.' Or, it would be better to say that God is simply 'the.' "

"The?"

"The. A great spiritual force. We have no quarrel with any other religion. Each has its place in the evolving spiritual understanding. However, we believe we have advanced beyond the teaching of most Christians, and in a few years our beliefs will be worldwide.

69

Many will follow us into this spiritual age, although we will not impose our views on anyone."

"In what way, then, does this God—or the—relate to your spirit forces?"

"I draw insight from the great spiritual force. But that force is too great for us to approach. We can't go to it. So we go to the cosmic forces. They transmit messages to us. Let me give you an example. When I first started, I received my instruction on when to open this church and how to conduct the meetings. At first we took up no collections. Now the forces have led me to take up collections. I obey the forces. If I do anything to disobey them, they will be taken away from me. And that I do not want. I prize this knowledge above everything else. I won't do anything to disobey these forces."

It almost seemed to me that spiritism is devoid of trust in God. As we talked it became clear that this distrust leads to spiritism, to approach other forces rather than God. Does all this mean that God is an afterthought instead of the ground of eternal life for man? I did not suggest these thoughts to her, but I asked: "Is there any other major difference between your beliefs and basic Christianity, as you see it?"

"Well, for one thing there is astral travel," she commented. "This means that my spirit leaves my body and travels to another plane. It's a little like sleeping and dreaming in your sleep. In my own experience I have spiritually traveled to the River Jordan and seen it. When I become very depressed I think of this vision. It helps me. This is how spiritualism works. You see, we find much good in other religions, but spiritualism helps people where they are."

"But don't you think that many religions do this too? Didn't Jesus help people where they were?"

"Yes, but most religions have not developed to this fuller understanding of both reincarnation and the life beyond."

"You believe in reincarnation?"

"Most sincerely. Not every spiritualist does, of course, but most do. I know that I could not learn all the lessons I have to learn and experience in one lifetime."

"Then you think of life as a learning process, becoming better until you qualify for something or other?"

"Yes, exactly."

"Qualify to become a cosmic force?"

"Yes."

"Have you ever lived before?"

"This is my fourth life. At least my fourth."

"How do you know?"

"I just know. I have had many trials, many struggles. I have suffered much."

She opened the door a crack in our conversation to many hardships in her childhood and early twenties. She was partially handicapped, and this must have been extremely painful for her to bear, since she was otherwise a pleasing and charming woman. I did not push the matter.

"I have had many struggles in life," she repeated. "I hope this is my last, for I have awakened spiritually. I feel a closeness with nature, so that I silently commune within my own consciousness."

"How do you evaluate death?"

My question seemed abrupt, but it went right to the heart of things.

71

"There is no death," she said at once. "We just pass from one expression to another. Since I have had glimpses of the other world, or rather just a tiny part of it, I know that it is very beautiful. Even beyond words to explain. We must work out our own destiny. We always receive what we earn, both good and bad. We can only erase some of our debts by good deeds and serving others."

Now she was speaking of a reliance on works. Not trust in the mercy of God. I wanted to make sure that I had understood her.

"I noticed a picture of Jesus here," I said. "What do you think of Jesus?"

"Jesus was a human being. He had divine faith in God which we do not have. He was the greatest spiritualist ever. He came to show us the way."

"Was Jesus more than a man?"

"He was the one who came from God. He set an example for us to follow. He was gifted with divine powers direct from God. *We* have to go through the cosmic forces, until we reach that state of perfection where we can communicate directly. He didn't have to."

"I also noticed a cross on the wall beside the picture. What does this cross mean to you?"

"He suffered as we all suffer. But we have to pay for everything we do, good or bad, until we work it out."

"Then you do not believe that He took our sins on Himself, or died for our sins? Christianity traditionally teaches this about the cross."

"No. We pay for our own sins as we go along. We pay for our sins in the next life, when we come back

72

to earth. I am now paying for the sins of my previous existence."

"To me that isn't much salvation," I said directly. "Besides it doesn't make me think kindly toward God, all this pay-as-you-go plan. Maybe an *it* or a *force* or *the* could hand me such a bum deal, but not the heavenly Father. A *father* would not do this. And God is our Father, who sent His Son into the world. . . ."

"Yes," she said. "Love is the triumphant power in the universe, but it all depends on how you interpret the Bible. You have to work out your own salvation. Now, the Bible is mostly parables. For example, I do not accept Judgment Day as it is in the Bible. I think that's a parable. There is no hell or anything like that. So also the suffering of Jesus is much like the suffering we endure."

"I want to ask you another question about Jesus, which seems central to our discussion about life and death. What about the Resurrection?"

"I believe in that."

"You do?"

"Yes."

I now made my point: "If you believe that Jesus actually rose from the dead, why then do we need to communicate with other forces to tell us about life and death? If *He* is alive forevermore and has ascended to the right hand of God. . . ."

She broke in: "Oh, but I don't believe in the traditional interpretation of the Resurrection. He was resurrected in a spiritual form. Not bodily. I see many spirit forces all about us. As I told you, *anyone* can become a cosmic force. Jesus was no different, really."

If only there had been an acceptance of the biblical

Resurrection, how vastly different the picture would be.

"These spirit forces are here now, even while we are talking. They are with us," she concluded.

She wanted to draw me into a further exploration of psychic phenomena, but I was not interested. After all, if Jesus had risen from the dead to bring life and immortality to light, what would be the point of tuning in to forces or voices? Do we need such reassurance, now that the revelation has been given for which the disciples sacrificed their lives?

At this point our conversation ended, and as I left her, I concluded that spiritualism was actually *unnecessary!* Faith in eternal life does not rest on the miraculous testimony through psychic mediums, but on the shattering victory of Jesus Christ from the dead.

When the resurrection of Jesus is not accepted as fact, the fear of the unknown leads to all sorts of substitutes. Man has always been curious about death. But only truth can expel error. Only fact can overcome fiction. Any so-called messages from the dead are poor and tawdry sideshows in comparison with the One who lived and is "alive for evermore," who says He has "the keys of Death and Death's domain," and whose assured promise is "because I live, you too will live" (Revelation 1:18; John 14:19).

SUMMARY
The Escapist

The word "beyond" may summarize the escape
artists. They all attempt to move beyond the conventional. The rebel has run away from the establishment,
the faddist has trekked beyond the historic faith and
the spiritualist travels beyond the veil of death.

How can we reach the escapist?

The rebel can only be reached when we identify
ourselves as rebels too. We are all prodigals who
have left the Father's house. Yet even there in that
far country, we remember our home. This memory
can shake us awake. We can feel sorry for ourselves.
We can run to a psychiatrist. We can stubbornly

continue in our reactionary behavior. Or we can return to the Father's house. It's up to every rebel.

The faddist needs to anchor to that faith which is historic and realistic. He must not allow himself to be blown about with every new teaching. He needs to discover for himself that which was declared from the beginning of the world, that his faith and hope may be in God.

The spiritualist who faces the uniqueness of the resurrection of Jesus, will no longer look beyond the veil of death. That veil has been torn apart. That barrier has been smashed by the actual resurrection of Jesus. Truth alone will end all speculation in the occult.

If only the escapee had a bit more realism, he would listen to the revelation of God in Christ. If only the good news could be accepted as truth, he would not remain on the lookout for the new, the bizarre and the illusory. If only. . . .

INTRODUCTION TO

THE MILITANT

Man is a military animal.
Glories in gunpowder and loves a parade.
PHILIP BAILEY

Some religious groups are divisive. They proceed from the premise that they alone possess the truth. On occasion Christianity has also been accused of being exclusive, particularly those who are orthodox, evangelistic and missionary-minded.

Now, there is a uniqueness in the Judeo-Christian tradition which cannot be avoided. It began with the call of Abraham and led to the concept of the chosen people, who were to bring a Messiah into the world. Jesus is declared to be the only begotten Son of God. He came, taught, died, and rose from the dead. Then He gave His disciples this final charge: "Go forth therefore and make all nations my disciples; baptize men everywhere" (Matthew 28:19).

But this is not to be considered a claim to exclusiveness. God entered the world. He expressed His love for every man in Jesus Christ. And this is the obvious result—a mission into all the world. Universal in scope and all-encompassing in compassion. "The real light which enlightens every man" has come (John 1:9). And the invitation is that "everyone who has faith in him may not die but have eternal life" (John 3:16).

The militant faiths I describe in the next three chapters march into the world with banners flying

79

and often swords flashing. Each claims to be the **only** way. Each has the truth. All others are false. Each demands total subjection. All others will be excluded from the rewards of heaven.

The Muslim faith has been traditionally militant. Although I talked with a spokesman for Islam, I also interviewed a militant black leader, whose message turned out to be not as religious as it was cultural. His approach to the racial situation is of vast importance. He is a representative of a growing community, which is becoming increasingly militant.

The Mormon mission representative whose task it was to missionize, was very precise and emphatic. He had the truth and it was the only truth. Those who acknowledge the revelation given to Joseph Smith and the authority of the Church of the Latter-day Saints receive the light and obtain the highest rewards.

I also spoke with two Jehovah's Witnesses. They claim to be the chosen few. They alone represent Jehovah to this generation. Their major task is to witness and awaken all men before the final battle of Armageddon.

There are surely other militant groups in the world, but these seem to be the most significant.

CHAPTER 7

The Black Muslim

The building was painted black. The doors were a fire-engine red. The inside was a gaudy chartreuse. The three colors represented the national colors of Africa. But black dominated everywhere—a symbol of racial pride.

The office looked rather bare, except for the pictures of the leader of the organization all over the walls, along with newspaper clippings of his activities. Two fellows moved about the office like cats, cleaning and rearranging, though it was after ten in the morning. By eleven a couple of secretaries had entered and were furiously typing away. The men still shuffled about, rearranging papers and making phone calls. The place was not unfriendly. I felt a mood of quiet determination.

One sign caught my immediate attention. "Just Trying to Be Black." This motto was carried on briefcases, which of course were black also. They were saying that they were tired of feeling that black was nothing, until it joined the white community. Black is something. For as I was later told: "Since we can't wash white, we should be proud to be black. We're simply trying to be ourselves. It's nothing to be ashamed of."

Most of the men wore beards, goatees or mustaches. They were of all descriptions. The vice-president, whom I interviewed, had a Mongolian-looking mustache, two wisps of hair beginning above either side of his mouth, which fell down straight in the fashion of Genghis Khan. He sat behind a desk, flanked by a few books—mostly on black power. His swivel chair creaked every time he shifted position, and he kept on forming his hands into triangle after triangle while we talked. He had mastered his doctrines and they flowed from him as a fountain spurts forth water freely.

"We are really a black, nationalist, cultural organization. We believe that the problem of the black community is a lack of values. We have no history, no background. Our history got lost in your history books and often it was misrepresented. We need a sense of values. Black people hate to admit that they have no culture. Every other group has. But we have one, too. And when we go back into Africa, we discover our art and music and heritage. This will give us a common bond, an ethos."

He stopped a moment to shift gears.

"But our American history," he continued, "comes from Christianity. And Christianity did not give us a concept but a *complex*. We are a cursed people. This is our main problem. We started off wrong, here, in America."

I broke in. "What do you mean 'cursed'? That is one particular interpretation of Christianity. And a very poor one, I might add."

"You people say that the Bible cursed Ham, Noah's son, and that's the curse on all blacks. I can't buy that."

"Neither can I," I said. "Look. When you read the Bible, you discover that the curse wasn't on Ham, but on Canaan. And then you find out that the Canaanites were the people that went into the land the Israelites later conquered. They couldn't have been black. The Promised Land wasn't in Africa."

"I've never heard that interpretation."

"Look it up for yourself. It's in Genesis 9 and 10."

"Well, anyway, that's the reality we're faced with," he countered. He was leaning forward now, his face alive, his hands freely drawing triangles on the desk. "We look at it this way. A God should do at least three things for people. He deals with them historically. He benefits them. And He looks like them. On those three counts Christianity has failed us—at least the way we've been presented with it."

"But that's the point," I said. "The way you've been *presented* with it. What if it's the wrong way? What if that interpretation is mistaken?"

"Even if it is," he continued, "that's the way it is. Christianity has done nothing for us. Jesus didn't either. Instead of freeing us, He put us in a bind. He put down certain morals which people can't follow."

"What do you mean?"

"Abstract morals. Negative commandments."

"Give me an illustration."

"Thou shalt not kill. That states you should not do something, because if you do, you'll get this." His fist banged down on the desk. Hard. "We have no negative values. Only what you should do."

83

"All right. Let me ask you something. What of the positive way Jesus sums up the law? He tells us to love the Lord with all our heart, mind, and strength, and our neighbor as ourselves. That's not negative."

He squirmed. It was clear that he had not confronted that question before. So he switched the subject. "What do you mean by God?" he asked.

"Well, for one thing, the Creator. The one who made all things."

"Now, we say that the black people were always here. There is no beginning. No creation."

As he launched into a discussion of creation, we left the positive emphasis of Jesus behind. We left it, because it would have demolished his reasons for rejecting the ethics of Jesus.

"We look at creation differently," he was saying now. "In the beginning were the black people."

"Why the black?"

"Anthropology confirms that. The first remains of man were found in Africa. It's the cradle of civilization. Africa had a culture before white men learned how to get along with each other. We are trying to apply all this to our experience in America. We can't play it white any more, so we're going to play it black."

"If you don't believe in a Creator God, do you believe in God at all?"

"Of course. If we were atheists, we wouldn't believe in ourselves. But man creates and man destroys. We take God out of the sky and put Him in our house. Each man is a god in his own house."

I didn't challenge him on this interpretation, but tried to bring the subject back: "You said a moment ago that you don't adhere to Christianity. . . ."

"No, because Christianity hasn't been good for us. Christianity has enslaved us. It was under Christianity in the Western world—and that is what we have to deal with—that everything has been done against black people."

"But what of the help Christians have given to Africa?"

That infuriated him.

"*What* help?" He raised his voice. "Africa is in bad shape. Christianity came with the cross. The missionary, the mercenary and the military. When the missionary put everybody's mind up in the sky, the mercenary exploited the land, and when the people woke up, the military controlled them. Christianity hasn't benefited the black people at all. Slavery isn't a very pleasant word, but you made slaves of us. Don't forget it. We can't. We came over here on the good ship 'Jesus.' "

I remained calm.

"I understand," I said. "I have no excuses. Nothing to say. Even to apologize. . . ."

"Apologies!" he burst out. "It's too late for apologies. Apologies don't say anything. We can't rely on you any longer. We can't believe you any more."

"Does this make you hate *all* white people?"

He calmed down a little.

"It would be flattering to hate white people," he said flatly. "We don't want to waste our energies like that. We are a peaceful people. We'd rather make love than war. So we address ourselves to establishing an alternative value system to the Western way of life. A completely new ideology. We don't hate white people, we just love black. And if we happen to look over white people, well, you know—*tough*. They've looked over us for centuries!"

"I had lunch with a friend who is a fine Negro," I interjected. "He said that at one end of the Negro community are the elite and at the other the militant. And he found himself moving toward the militant side, although a few years ago he considered himself more of the elite. It surprised me, because he holds a responsible managerial position and represents the very best of your people."

"It shouldn't surprise you," he said coolly. "That's the way it's moving."

"Doesn't all this have a parallel to the Muslim faith? Doesn't the Koran teach the followers of Mohammed to use the sword?"

"That's true, but the Koran doesn't teach that anyone can be forced into Islam. The son is not to follow the father because the father forces him."

"And Muslims also reject Christians. Why?"

"Muslims think that to go back into Christianity is to step backwards. Islam believes all the messengers of God, including Jesus, but the *last* of these gives the most advanced teaching. And that is Mohammed. Since Mohammed was the last messenger of God, Islam is the completion of all religions."

"Would you say that Mohammed founded a political as well as a religious community?"

"That's true. In the Koran obedience to God and to the Prophet are inseparably linked. That includes the use of the sword when necessary."

"Perhaps that explains the militancy of the Black Muslims."

"Yes," he said, steadily forming triangles on the desk

between us. "They are nationalists. But they have their own interpretation of Islam."

"In what way are they different?"

"Well, Mohammed left no set way for religion to be practiced. That gives them liberty. But I suppose the big difference is that there are white people in Islam; not among the Black Muslims. They say Islam is the black man's religion."

"How can that be?"

"Well, it isn't true, of course."

He was well versed in Islam, but his emphasis lay in this new country with its new problems and needs. And yet I wanted to establish the connection.

"Do you believe in Mohammed?" I asked.

"I believe he was a prophet. He united a people and brought about an Arab civilization. Almost an empire. But this was for the Arabs. The true African religion and tradition is what we adhere to."

"But hasn't Islam made quite an impact on Africa? Doesn't it have many followers there?"

"Right. But then it was a religion which came from the outside. It did not originate there. We are dealing with African people and values. So we address ourselves to teaching these values to young people. We are not ashamed of being black."

I spoke again more from my feelings than my intellect: "I find it difficult to talk to you as a Christian."

"Well, I'm not against Christianity," he broke in. "For *you*. It's good for you. But for us it's no good."

"What do you think of Jesus?"

"He was a good man. A prophet."

"What of His claim that He is the Son of God?"

"Well, I'd have to go along with the Muslim religion

there. They say that the references to Jesus as the Son of God were added by Christians. I don't believe that God needed to be brought down in the form of a man. God does not need a son. The Christian incarnation is too materialistic an idea."

"We Christians affirm that Jesus came to die for the sin of the world," I said. "What about the meaning of the crucifixion?"

"You know that Muslims don't believe Jesus was crucified," he replied immediately. "It appeared to people that He was. God took Jesus to Himself without His dying. He never was put upon the cross."

"Then, who died on the cross?"

"Judas. He was punished for betraying Jesus. So, when Jesus supposedly was raised from the dead, He wasn't. He had not yet died. The Koran glorifies Jesus so much that He did not need to sacrifice Himself. No, He did not take away the sin of the world. No one can be punished for our mistakes. We only are responsible for our sins."

Since he was handing me the orthodox Muslim line, I returned again to his main interest.

"Did you imply a moment ago that when you said Christianity is only good for us, that it isn't right for the black community?"

He reiterated his position: "Right. It only works for white people. Nobody else benefits from it."

"But what of the black community that embraces Christianity? Aren't there many Negroes who are Christians?"

"They're misguided blacks. We say to them, 'Look what you're faced with; what answers do you come up with?' They're Christians because of habit. They've been going to church for so long. Or they're afraid to change. So, we put the emphasis on the young people and forget about them."

"And Martin Luther King's beliefs . . . ?"

"His ideas are not up to date. Look at this nonviolent approach. It got him killed. I would rather *not* fight anybody. But we have to move in self-defense. We believe in power, black power. If we have it, we won't have to worry about any man kicking in our door. The difference between the black people and the Jewish people is that the Jewish people have power. The police don't kick their doors down, because they can bring pressure to bear. Blacks are subject to anything, because we have no power."

"Aren't you aware that many whites are concerned about this? Remember the tribute to Martin Luther King? Thousands of us want to change conditions as much as you do."

"We agree that all white people don't take the same attitude," he said leaning forward. "And we would like to see white people give us some aid in terms of resources, technical help, jobs, better housing and so on. Then if they'd go into their own communities and through constructive programs avoid this coming violence. We can't wait for words. We want change. We've got to play it black. We're militant."

We parted in mutual concern. I tried again to express my personal interest, and he seemed to accept it. It was my hope to establish some sort of communication, some bridge of understanding.

I could not raise more questions about Christianity, for he dismissed them either with the Muslim religion or the race issue. The previous question would have to be settled first, the question of race prejudice which had humiliated the black man, the question of inequality which had created such a wide gulf, and above all the question of slavery which still smarts and burns in the black community.

How can that wound ever be healed? How can Christianity regain a people it once enslaved, and even now relegates to second class? These are the questions which must lead Christians to confession first, before any avenues can be opened to fruitful communication. Certainly the perversion of the white man's Christianity has been totally out of step with Jesus Christ.

CHAPTER 8
The Mormon

After several phone calls and some hesitation on his part, I was able to see the official representative of the growing and active Church of Jesus Christ of Latter-day Saints.

"I'm a businessman who is losing money by being here," he informed me. "But I was called, and so I am in this office."

He gave his time freely to the church, without pay, as do all twelve thousand who actively work as missionaries. But I had to convince him that my desire to exchange views was genuine. After breaking down some initial barriers, we talked frankly, and it soon brought into focus the glaring differences between us.

He was a kindly, yet reserved man in his fifties.

He seemed very sincere, and yet at times he sounded to me like a machine, spitting out information. The dogma was Mormon and he believed it profoundly. I did not always feel it was personally his. But when I questioned him on it, he said it was, and he said it earnestly.

His office looked tidy and efficient. He impressed me as a top businessman, for he mentioned that his entire business had burned down a couple of years earlier and was now rebuilt, so that he was able to give his full time to the church. He smiled when he spoke, but he was cautious at first. Open in a reserved way, until he felt free to rush me with missionary vigor.

I started off by asking him: "What in essence is it that you're trying to say to the world?"

His answer was immediate: "To be united."

I asked him to explain.

"To base everything upon truth. We teach the plan of salvation. We proclaim to the individual, whom we believe is a god in embryo, and therefore can become like God, that he is to obey the laws which God Himself obeys."

"God obeys His laws?"

"Of course! That's what makes Him God. He would not be God, if He did not obey His laws. God becomes God as He obeys truth."

"Does that not make the law greater than the One who gives the law?"

"God has become God because He has gained intelligence. God is a man with body and parts and passions, as we are. He is as you and I."

"Then God is not eternally God? Not eternally perfect and holy?"

"No. He *became* perfect. The difference between man and God is in the degree of intelligence. We can become like Him, and that's what He wants us to do. That is also how God progresses. He progresses through us, as a father progresses through his children. One of our first presidents, Lorenzo Snow, put it like this: 'As man is, God once was. As God is, man may become.' "

"Then man is not created in the image of God?"

"We are built as He," he answered smoothly. "We look like Him. And He had a Son, who became the God of this earth. We also will become gods of other earths. It is a great incentive for me to become smart enough so that I will be able to govern others with justice and truth. Like God. I think it's a beautiful concept."

He was wound up now and I let him continue talking about his beliefs of God and man.

"We came into this world with the intelligence we earned in a preexistence," he intoned. "We were created spiritually before we came into mortality. We leave this earth with the added intelligence we gain."

"We had intelligence before we came here?"

"Oh, yes!"

"Where did it come from?"

"From another earth, where we existed before we came here. I believe you agreed to come here at this time."

"How do you know?"

"I can't prove it. Only, I know it by the spirit which dictates to me that this is the truth."

It was obvious we were already miles apart in our concepts of God and man. We could have argued long

93

about these beliefs, but all this was built on something else. So I did not challenge these views, but proceeded to the foundation. Why did he hold these ideas? Where did they come from? I switched to that subject: "Do you think that The Church of Jesus Christ of Latter-day Saints has brought something new into the world?"

"I quote from Jesus," he answered. " 'If it had been the church of Moses, I would have called it Moses. But you can identify my church by the name that it carries.' "

"Where are you quoting from?"

"Out of the Book of Mormon."

"Not the words of Jesus from the Bible?"

"No."

He realized that I would not accept that quotation as authentic, but he continued. "Our church has brought about a restoration, restoring those things that needed to be restored: authority, the priesthood, obedience to the law, a prophet who represents God's truth. It is inconceivable that God would have more than one prophet at a time."

"Why?"

"There could not be order then. Justice could not prevail."

"In the history of Israel, for example, Isaiah and Amos were prophets at the same period."

"Who was the true prophet?" he asked.

"Both seem to have made it into the Bible," I said.

He switched the subject: "There were popes in Rome and in France at the same time. There are many protestant denominations. Which is the true one? We have to have order. Somewhere there must be full authority."

"Then you are saying that God works today through the one prophet of The Church of Jesus Christ of Latter-day Saints?"

"Right. Our president in Salt Lake City."

"What about the Pope?"

"The Pope is out of it. We believe all Christendom will come into The Church of Jesus Christ of Latter-day Saints. They will see the truth, for not only have the prophets been restored, but the apostles and the priesthood also. Both the Melchizedek and the Aaronic priesthood."

He was all wound up, explaining the church.

"It is my personal belief that God came down to a young man, and in one fell swoop showed Himself and said, 'This is My beloved son, hear him.' There He delegated authority to this uneducated fellow, on how to write a new witness—and that is the Book of Mormon."

"You're talking about Joseph Smith?"

"Yes."

"And God said to him the same words which He said to Jesus, 'This is My beloved Son; hear Him' "?

"Yes. And that settles the question that God has a body, parts and passions."

I passed by his last remark. I wanted to get his perspective on how God could have worked *only* through Joseph Smith, and not, for example, through the Reformers.

He explained that the church had passed through the Dark Ages, lost the true version of the Bible and forgot the authority God intended for it. In short, the church became apostate. As for the Reformation and Luther and Calvin: "They were tremendous teachers.

But they did not have the authority. That's the key to the whole thing. God's authority can only be delegated to one prophet at a time. There must be order. The Reformation was a protest. It was necessary. But it was not a *restoration*."

"Now, if it is true that authority has been restored through Joseph Smith, can you accept other Christians?"

"We don't agree, do we?" he asked candidly. "We don't agree on our concepts of God and man." I nodded to indicate I was quite aware of our differences. "So how can there be unity? I cannot give in to that which is contrary to the truth! There can be no such thing as merging with all Christians."

"Then the unity you spoke of at the beginning of our conversation was not a unity for all Christians, but for all men to come to the official church, the Mormon Church."

"That's right. The recognition of the delegated authority and the truth. You see, Mormonism is Christianity and Christianity is Mormonism."

"By the way, where does this word 'Mormon' come from?"

"Mormon was the ancient Nephite prophet who compiled the sacred records of his people. This became the Book of Mormon, which Joseph Smith discovered."

He now brought out a handsomely bound copy of the Book of Mormon, placed it alongside his Bible and patted it with admiration.

"This becomes a *second* witness. It was needed. The Book of Mormon is the word of God. The Bible is the Word of God insofar as it is translated correctly."

"Does that mean there are mistakes in the Bible?"

"Yes. Through translations. I can show you many errors."

"And no mistakes in the Book of Mormon?"

"No mistakes. Joseph Smith said that it is the most correct of any book on earth."

"Does this place the Book of Mormon in a superior position to the Bible?"

He switched again. "Wouldn't you think," he asked and his missionary passion was now coming forth steadily, "that there would be a need for a straightening out and correction, if there were many versions of the Bible and errors?"

"You proceed on a basis I can't accept. I don't see a need for correction, for that assumes all Christianity has gone astray," I replied. "But more important, there would need to be harmony between the Bible and the Book of Mormon. And we have already seen conflicts. Furthermore, I find it incredibly difficult to accept the historic portions of the Book of Mormon, such as the tribes of Israel migrating to the United States before Christ."

"Have you seen the archeological evidence for it?"

"No."

"The many ruins?"

"No."

"I have held in my hands a brass plate which they say was similar to the ones on which the Book of Mormon was written."

"Do you actually possess the original plates?"

"No."

"Where are they?"

"With the angel Moroni."

I was thinking of artifacts and relics brought forth

as proof in another tradition, but I didn't say anything about that.

"Do you then identify yourselves with Israel?" I asked.

"Very much so. We add to the story. We tell Israel where the twelve tribes came from and who they really are."

"Who are they?"

"The Israelites are a portion of the twelve tribes. We are the descendents from the house of Ephraim, Judah and Manasseh."

"You are descendents of the Jews?"

"Right."

He was leaning forward now and very eager. He did not feel that he was being questioned. He seemed rather confident that he was going to question me and pursue the possibility of reaching me for his church. It was his job, after all.

I raised a leading question.

"What will happen to those who do *not* become Mormons, and will not accept the Book of Mormon?"

"Their capacity to become gods will be restricted. Take temple marriage, for example. Unless you're married in the temple, you will not be sealed to your family for time and eternity. That is one ordinance which must be obeyed."

He had again contradicted the clear teaching of Jesus. This time on marriage and heaven. Now he said: "Your exposure places you in a more precarious position. You have been warned. I have sincerely attempted to teach you."

"You're communicating," I said and he laughed. It relieved the tension somewhat, but he felt even more free to stalk, as if he were hunting big game.

"Let me ask you just a simple question," he proceeded eagerly. "If you knew that the Saviour had been on earth and had reestablished His church, as He promised He would . . ."

"Where did He promise that?" I broke in.

"He promised it many times. But, if it were true, would you be interested?"

If it were true, I weighed his words.

"All right, that's all I want to know. Then you will listen to what we have to teach?"

"If it is true. . . ." I repeated. "But you will have to convince me from Scripture that Jesus promised to reestablish His church."

He picked up the Bible and started thumbing through. It took him a bit of time. I waited. He kept fumbling. Finally, I broke the silence.

"Are you open to reject *your* position?" I asked.

He didn't answer.

"Suppose the evidence is on the other side? Not with you, but in the mainstream of evangelical Christianity?"

"I would want truth wherever it is."

Luckily he found something and started to read: "I know that my redeemer liveth, and that he shall stand at the latter day upon the earth" (Job 19:25, K.J.V.).

"Yes, that's from Job," I said. "It expresses Job's personal faith in the resurrection. What has this to do with reestablishing the church?"

He now closed the Bible and said: "We believe the second coming has taken place."

"Has it? Did Jesus establish the Kingdom of God? Did every eye see Him? Did all the tribes of the earth mourn? Did the dead in Christ rise? Was there a universal judgment? All this is in Scripture. You cannot by any stretch of the imagination find fulfillment of the second coming of Christ in one single revelation to Joseph Smith!"

"It fulfills the promise of the other sheep. . . ."

I threw more cold water on his missionary zeal.

"Jesus said that, about the sheep, to the Jewish apostles. The sheep would be gathered from the Gentiles, from all over the world. You cannot appropriate that exclusively to the Mormons."

"Yes, you can turn it almost any way you want to," he said quietly. "But I believe the Joseph Smith story."

"Tell me what you really think about Jesus," I said.

"Jesus was the Son of God. A literal Son with a spiritual Father and temporal mother. We believe the virgin birth. He grew as a normal boy."

"Is there a specific significance to the death of Jesus?"

"Yes. He took the sins of men by laying down His life. He showed us how to follow Him and do what He did."

"Are you forgiven because of His death on your behalf?"

"No. He gives us the opportunity to save ourselves."

"How are you forgiven then?"

"By our actions." He repeated it softly. "By our actions. The atonement was by plan. Jesus was the first one to lay down His life. He gave the supreme sacrifice. We are saved by grace *and* by works."

"Doesn't that presuppose some kind of achievement on the part of man? Does man deserve heaven because of his achievements?"

"He makes heaven by the grace of God *and* by his achievement. He gets more for his works, his use of intelligence, his spiritual growth."

"Is there salvation outside The Church of Jesus Christ of Latter-day Saints?"

"No, there can't be. Without the atonement, the priesthood, the authority and the sealing power there can be no salvation."

All the time in spite of his gracious ways, he was laying more bricks into the wall which grew up between us.

"It all hinges on Joseph Smith, doesn't it?" I asked again.

"Oh, of course! If you can't believe the Joseph Smith story, then there's nothing. I don't think God would come to Calvin or Luther. They had ideas of their own. Joseph Smith wasn't smart enough. It had to be a revelation. Look. If this vision was but a figment of Joseph Smith's imagination, then the Mormon church is a fraud. If it were true, we are the exclusive church of Jesus Christ in these latter days."

"This makes Joseph Smith the most important person in history, since Jesus Christ. Doesn't it?"

"The most important person since Jesus Christ!" He underlined the words. "There's no question about it."

Well, there it was. We could have argued doctrines all day, but it came back to the restoration, the revelation given to Joseph Smith. That or nothing. He told me that I'd have to be very humble to throw aside all my learning and be open to the teaching of the true church. He was ever the aggressive, smiling missionary. A man sincerely convinced and convincing.

I told him that I believed in the finality of Hebrews

1:1,2: "God . . . in this the final age . . . has spoken to us in the Son." This was God's supreme revelation of Himself. There was no need for any other. Nor can anyone rise above Jesus Christ, the only begotten Son of God, the eternal Word made flesh.

Besides, the phrase "in these last days" refers to the incarnation of Jesus. Not to the period beginning with Joseph Smith. "Days" in biblical thinking can extend for many years, for a day is as a thousand years. So the clear teaching of Scripture is that the last days began with the coming of Christ.

My words seemed to have fallen on deaf ears. The wall was in place. We had piled up too many bricks. And only a miracle of grace could demolish it.

CHAPTER 9

The Jehovah's Witness

It was late Saturday morning and I was working on the lawn, when he came by with his wife and children. After his first sentence I knew that he was a Jehovah's Witness. I immediately cut him off. "I really don't have time to talk with you today, but I want to speak with the leader of your local group."

I explained who I was, and why I was eager for a conversation. He told me he was the leader and was very willing to explain his beliefs to me. A couple of weeks later we sat down in his living room, and he informed me that the Witnesses have extended themselves into about two hundred countries and covered most of their populations house to house. In fact, the United States is regularly canvassed four times a year, which is a creditable task for less than 350,000 ardent Witnesses. (They have over a million in the world.)

He had asked another member of his congregation

to listen and add moral support. So there we sat face-to-face in his simple, but comfortable living room, while a warm fire glowed in the fireplace.

He immediately enlightened me that the three main doctrines of Christianity which they could not accept were the Trinity, the immortality of the soul and hellfire. The Trinity was pagan, the immortality of the soul would mean that man did not need to receive eternal life and the Bible teaches annihilation, not hell.

"We recognize the Bible as the instrument of the will of God," he stated as a premise. "Not in a fundamentalistic sense, though. Some passages are to be taken literally and others symbolically."

"Well," I said. "Here's a case in point. I've heard Witnesses say that they are the 144,000. Is this an actual or a symbolic number?"

"This is an absolute number. These are the sheep of which Jesus speaks."

"Aren't there already *more* than 144,000 Witnesses in the world?"

"Yes. The Bible says there are other sheep—John 10:16. So these will include those Witnesses who are not in the original 144,000."

He always quoted Bible verses to back up every point.

"Interpretation belongs to God," he pointed out. He had just given me a most curious one of the 144,000. The number is symbolic, twelve times twelve times a thousand. One twelve represents the tribes of Israel, the other the apostles. This is multiplied to perfection by a thousand. The number represents the Old and New Testaments united, Jews and Christians as believers.

104

But he was going on: "Just as Joseph said about the dreams of Pharaoh—Genesis 40:8—no man can interpret the Bible without the Spirit. Therefore, we, the modern-day society of His worshipers can truly interpret Scripture."

"You call yourselves the modern-day society of His worshipers?"

"Right. Because there are three distinct time periods in this arrangement. Abel was the first witness—Hebrews 11:4. Jesus was the chief witness, Revelation 1:5. We fulfill the prophecy of Isaiah 43:10: 'Ye are my witnesses.' As the true followers of Jehovah, we call ourselves by that name."

"If that is true, then what happened between the early days of Christianity and the twentieth century? Were there true Christians in apostolic days?"

"Oh, yes. In fact, some of those are among the 144,000."

"Then what happened in those 1900 years?"

"You remember how Peter said that wolves would enter in—II Peter. . . ."

"Yes."

"This, of course, happened at the Council of Nicaea."

"Of course? You don't accept the Nicene Creed?"

"Definitely not."

"And the Apostles' Creed?"

"No. This creed was a formation of men, not the apostles. The Bible says that all this would take place, that Christendom would become apostate, believe in folklore and myths, and substitute men's philosophies for the truth."

He stopped a moment.

"That's why Jehovah had to raise up the Witnesses,"

he said pointedly. "Let God be true and all men liars—Romans 3:4."

We started to talk about Jesus. He brought up a great passage (Philippians 2:5–11), from which he attempted to point out that since Jesus humbled Himself, He was not equal with God, or "a part of the Trinity," as he put it.

I took up the passage: "These verses say that Jesus is Lord. He humbled Himself unto death, even the death of the cross, but He is highly exalted in resurrection. Every knee shall bow to Him and every tongue confess His Lordship. Do you accept this?"

"Definitely." He paused. Then he added a qualifying statement. "Of course you have to know what the word 'Lord' means."

"What do you mean by it?"

"Well—owner and master."

"Not the Lord God?"

"No. You could be a lord over slaves."

"But the passage speaks of the risen Lord. He is given a name above every name. He is exalted above all others."

"Right. The Lord as Spirit.creature."

"What do you mean by that?"

"Jesus died. He went out of existence. Then He became alive in the Spirit, as Peter testified. I Peter 3:18. This was a higher type of life than you and I are experiencing."

"Then you do not believe in His physical resurrection?"

"No."

Since he was using Scripture, I thought I would bring up a passage: "What do you make of Jesus' appearance to Thomas, which is recorded in John 20? Jesus showed him His wounds."

"Right. There are various accounts like this. After His death the morale of the disciples was at a low ebb. Jesus appeared in a form to give them this assurance. He assumed a manifested body."

"But He ate with His disciples after His resurrection. He said He was *not* a ghost."

"Yes. But let's shift our minds to Genesis 6. Here we also have manifested angelic creatures. They come to the earth. They do things that men can do. They have children. In a similar way, as the angels assumed human manifestations, Jesus used different bodies. He was simply a materialized angel!"

"May I repeat what I think you're telling me?" I failed to see any real connection between Genesis 6 and the risen Lord.

"All right," they said. "It will help us, too."

"You are trying to say that Jesus died and rose in a spirit form. This spirit form was able to assume bodily shape."

"Right."

"Then what happened to His body?"

"It was destroyed."

"How?"

"God took those elements and removed them. Jesus received immortality. A transfer to another form of life. And, you see, if He received immortality, He could not have had it. He was not eternal. That's why we don't accept the Trinity."

"What do you make of John 17:5? Jesus Himself said that He had glory with the Father *before the world was.*"

"We believe that," he said firmly. "But we know He was a created being. We know Jesus to be Michael, the archangel, from Daniel 12:1."

"I fail to grasp the connection."

"You see, He had great glory with the Father before the world. He was the primary one in the chain of command, the chief angel who appeared in the Old Testament. Therefore He is a creation of the Father, an angelic creature."

"So, you are saying that Jesus was a created angel who came to earth and now has received immortality?"

"Exactly. And we will share with Him in this elevation. The 144,000 will also be spirit creatures. What more could we desire than to reign as kings and priests?"

I couldn't help but interject something.

"Do you realize this was considered a heresy by the Christian church in the fourth century, when a man named Arius advanced it?"

"No, I didn't know that."

He looked slightly bewildered, but he made a quick recovery.

"This is why we won't accept the church's creeds," he said.

"Is it fair to point out that your definition of the resurrection is not the same as historic Christianity?"

"Very definitely. You should point it out," he said emphatically. "Because it *isn't*."

"Now, what if the interpretation of historic Christianity happens to be correct, and there was a bodily resurrection of Jesus Christ? What would this do to your doctrines?"

He worked around the question. He repeated his

theories. He didn't really answer my questions, which didn't seem to bother him as much as a sonic boom rattling windows. But he did throw in a remark about the ransom theory, which states that Christ died for us. He didn't believe in it.

"What do you think Jesus accomplished by dying on the cross?" I asked.

He stumbled around for a few moments, so I made it more pointed: "Did Christ take away *your* sins by His death?"

"Yes," he said surprisingly enough, but then he modified it. "We have to qualify for it. We have to show our faith by our works."

"Do you have to work *for* your salvation, or are you living the Christian life *because of* your salvation?"

"You cannot work for your salvation."

"Then you are saved by faith."

"Yes."

"By faith alone?"

"By faith and works. James 2:14. Jesus' death does not guarantee you eternal life. It gives you a second chance for eternal life. If you are obedient as a witness of Jehovah. By works we mean going out and telling others. Romans 10. . . ."

"Therefore I would not qualify as a Christian if I did not become a Witness?" I broke in.

"That's right."

He also told me that works of social importance were not for this age. Building a hospital was not part of Jesus' instruction for the last days.

"Will people of other religions be saved?"

"No. Only the Witnesses will survive the battle of Armageddon."

"All others will be destroyed?" I asked.

"Of course. All nations who are against God and all apostate Christendom as seen in Revelation 17."

Here was the essence of their militant exclusivism. It could not have been more plain.

"How long have you been a Witness?" I asked.

"About ten years. Before that I was with the Churches of Christ."

"Were you active?"

"Definitely. But my close study of the Bible made quite a difference. I saw the light."

"Would you ever be willing to return to Protestantism?"

"There would be no way at all."

"You would not be open at all?"

"Very definitely not. Protestants represent one phase of that false religion which is under the control of the enemy."

"Even though leaders within Christianity affirm they serve God and not the devil?"

"Their works prove them to be different," he countered. "They are not doing God's will. Jesus said that not every one who calls Him 'Lord,' will enter the kingdom of heaven. Matthew 7:21."

"I accept those words of Jesus, too. I've preached on them. But how can you put *all* Christians into that category?"

"Because they are not witnesses of Jehovah."

"What about someone like Billy Graham? Is he an instrument of the devil?"

"Billy Graham is accomplishing something quite foreign to Bible Christianity. He is not an instrument of Christ."

110

"Have you personally heard him?" I inquired.

"Sure."

"Is he mistaken in his interpretation of the Bible?"

"I feel he doesn't have any interpretation of the Bible."

"What about the people who experience Christ and come forward at a Graham meeting? Their lives are dramatically changed."

"When religion is based on emotion it is a temporary thing," he said coolly.

"But a true experience, I mean. Suppose a person actually stops the drug habit and lives a clean life?"

"The devil can do miracles."

"You mean to say it is not the Holy Spirit when a person is converted, and you can see the evidence five years later?"

"Some of the most moral people in the world are atheists."

"But this addict or former alcoholic says that *Christ* has made him whole."

"It's not necessarily so. Men even die for false things. This is not the only explanation for it."

"Do you believe in the Holy Spirit?"

"Definitely. As the active force under God's control."

"Not as equal with God, the Spirit of God, the Trinity?"

"No."

"So you believe that the Spirit is working through the Witnesses, but never through Billy Graham."

"Yes. And in a different way than you imagine. Not through gifts. Only in getting the message preached worldwide."

111

"You don't believe in the gifts of the Spirit, such as healing or. . . ."

"Not for today."

"What of the greatest gift of all—love?"

"Oh. We have that. We have great love among ourselves. And we show our love for mankind by going door to door."

Our conversation seemed like a ride on a merry-go-round. It was amazing to watch him switch from one subject to another. Never did we pursue any major issue to its rightful conclusion. Through quotations of Scripture, generally out of context, he would turn to something else.

So everything was laid out. A system of beliefs with scriptural proofs for every point. Yet Scripture no longer spoke to the Witnesses. It was being quoted to prop up particular positions. And since he was at liberty to interpret some passages literally and others symbolically, he felt perfectly free to pick either category as it served the occasion.

We shook hands and I thanked him for his time. It was his pleasure, he said, but I sensed his relief that the conversation was finished.

It seems incredible that there are rational and decent people who believe that the Bible was written for the single purpose of proving that the Jehovah's Witnesses alone are right.

The Militant

At the conclusion of a banquet for foreign students, where I had spoken on Christianity and the world religions, the Muslim students ran forward at once to challenge. (We shall see in the next section why the Hindus and Buddhists were not disturbed.)

The Muslim religion has become Christianity's most stubborn adversary. That is because, like the Mormons and the Witnesses, Muslims think they have gone a step beyond Christianity. Any religion which claims that it holds the final truth, will not remain susceptible. There will always be a clash of ideas.

Yet in this clash of ideas is our hope. When the message of Christ is challenged by the Muslim or the black, questions will be raised. The Bible may be investigated. And those who will come to grips with the Scriptures, will find their way ultimately to Christ.

The Mormons read the Bible. But since they lay the Book of Mormon not only beside it, but actually in a superior position to it, their interpretation is colored by those revelations. Our only hope is to present the teaching of the Bible and thereby repudiate the spurious authority of the Book of Mormon. Has it ever occurred to members of The Church of Latter-day Saints that there are vast contradictions between Joseph Smith and Scripture?

The Jehovah's Witnesses have only the Word of God, but their slanted interpretations lead them astray. They construct a system of salvation by good works. We can only reason with a Jehovah's Witness if he is willing to listen to a more scholarly and historic, sane and truthful Christianity.

Perhaps only when the stubborn militant begins to fear he is losing the battle, will he become receptive to the ever new and better way.

Like a car in reverse, a closed mind is not open to new directions. Not until it moves from reverse into neutral is there a possibility of shifting into forward gear.

INTRODUCTION TO

THE TOLERANT

*It is not a merit to tolerate,
but rather a crime to be intolerant.*
SHELLEY

Just as the escapist is diametrically opposed to
the realist, so those who view religion with toleration
are at the other extreme from the militant. If the
militant religions are hard and exclusive, the tolerant
religions are soft and inclusive. Separationists divide
men from each other. Permissive people express the
universality of religious feelings and commonly
shared beliefs.

The Buddhist priest to whom I talked was very
permissive. He was broad about his beliefs. Even
though the religion of the Buddha had spread

throughout the Eastern world, he could hardly be termed a missionary. I also participated in a meditation service in a Zen Buddhist temple.

The Hindu faith is all-inclusive. According to the Hindu, whatever religion a person holds doesn't matter too much. Atheists and devout believers are both acceptable. They say that all rivers flow into the sea. My interview took me to an intelligent man who was born in India, educated in Great Britain and lives in the Western world as a modern, cultured mystic.

The Christian Scientist, and those like the Religious Scientist and others who ride piggyback on the movement, express a similar approach to religion. The very modern couple with whom I talked should give an insight into the tolerant and soft Science thinking.

CHAPTER 10

The Buddhist

A young man with a crew cut, barely thirty, wearing dark-rimmed glasses, greeted me as I entered the Buddhist Temple. A large, cold, concrete structure, located downtown in one of our big cities, it was served by seven priests; but John was the only one who spoke English.

He was not only able to discuss his faith. He also moved about easily in Western thought. He informed me that he had read such Jewish writers as Buber and Baeck, with whom he felt some kinship, and such Christian theologians as Barth and Tillich.

As we sat down to talk, he immediately took out

a pipe, which became an integral part of our conversation. He was as relaxed as the comfortable sport jacket and suede shoes he wore. As he smoked his pipe leisurely, his easy way of living harmonized with the almost matter-of-fact way in which he viewed his faith.

Though we represented two very different cultures, we almost at once accepted one another as persons. He smiled warmly and tried his best to give me direct answers. But the word that characterized both his faith and slow manner of speaking was the word "relaxed." And yet I noticed beneath this relaxed outward appearance, an inner nervousness. His hands shook ever so slightly. He made a conscious effort to keep himself controlled.

He explained that although he belonged to the largest sect of Buddhism in Japan, which had been in existence about seven hundred years, his thinking was basically and representatively Buddhist. Just as he was not interested to know whether I was a Methodist, a Presbyterian or a Baptist, but simply represented Christianity, so I proceeded to talk with him as a Buddhist.

"Do you think there is an interest in Buddhism in the Western world?" I asked John.

"Well, it's hard to say," he started. "Obviously on the surface there is. Some are more deeply interested in it. It's a recent phenomenon, if for no other reason than the translation of our scriptures into English."

"Are the so-called intellectuals studying Buddhism?"

"Yes, and on the college level. Certainly some want to know the teaching of the Buddha, and so there are many books about us. Publishers wouldn't put out books if they were not being read, but I would say most of them are trash. They're not worth reading, half of them anyway. They try to capitalize on popular approaches, reprinting stuff that has already been printed."

He had just returned from a visit to Japan, so I asked him about the influence of Buddhism there.

"Religiously speaking," he answered, "I would say there is a great desire on the part of the people for something, and they don't seem to find it in traditional religion."

"Billy Graham has just conducted meetings in Japan. What impact has his message had upon the nation?"

"If I am to believe the reports, there was an amazing response. Many people came. People are hungry for something. They will seek for anything."

I switched the subject to another interest of Western man and asked him about Zen Buddhism.

"Zen is actually a detailed way of meditation, through which people hope to achieve enlightenment. Zen is a way of reflecting on the actual conditions of our life and realizing the true meaning of the self."

"Why has it made some impact on people?"

"I would say that Zen differs from other Buddhist sects in that it emphasizes that every individual *is* Buddha. Meditation, which is the essence of Zen, is the way to achieve it. A Zen Buddhist once said to me that we are to learn our lessons. I tend to agree with that."

"It is easy to learn our lessons?"

A smile broke over his young face. It was a revealing smile. Learning one's lessons was evidently the hardest job of all. At least that is what he conveyed to me by his smile.

121

"What is really at the heart of your own beliefs?" I asked him.

He laughed nervously, leaned back, puffed on his pipe, and took his time. It was a question he had never faced before. He told me so later. It took him off guard. Certainly he knew what he believed, but what was the message of Buddhism for the world?

This is what he finally answered: "Well. I would ultimately have to go back to the formula of the four noble truths, that suffering is universal, that its cause is craving, that the cure for suffering is to eliminate this craving, and that we eliminate it by the eightfold path. You know, right beliefs, right intentions, right speech, right actions, and so on."

Only the memorized words came quickly. The remainder was painfully slow.

"I think, ultimately, the problem revolves around suffering—and the freedom from suffering."

"This is basically your message?"

"Right."

"Man suffers and wants to be free from it?"

"No. Man does not always *want* to be free. But Buddhism tries to teach me this. Man goes on in the world of suffering. But there is a situation where there is freedom from suffering. And because I have tasted this, there is a desire on my part to communicate it."

"If I were to ask you how I can achieve this freedom from suffering, what would you tell me?"

Again there was a long silence. He sat there thinking, taken aback by my practical questions, blowing smoke into the air and muttering to himself, "What must you do? What must you do . . . ?"

Then he said: "There is no pat answer. Buddhism

122

stands on the premise that there are eighty-four thousand ways, or, in other words, that there is a way for each person. His own way."

"May I ask you a specific question then?"

He nodded.

"Should the way include prayer?"

"No."

"Worship?"

"Not necessarily."

"Faith in God?"

"No."

"Is it a matter of discipline?"

"Only as a go-between."

"Is it something that comes to you, as I would define the grace of God?"

"Each sect in Buddhism is a different way. Some call it grace. We call it compassion. Compassion is given to us."

"From where?"

"From where?" he looked puzzled. He repeated it again. And he smiled. There was another pause. "From where?" he asked a third time. But he had no source for it.

There is a kind of grace or compassion in Buddhism, but it is really cheap grace. Cheap, because it doesn't cost anything. Besides, it is not given by God. There is no source for it. (The grace of God in Jesus Christ cost God an Incarnation and a Crucifixion!)

"We think of the absolute as infinite wisdom, infinite compassion," he now attempted to explain. "Because *it* is absolute, there is no way to relate to it. The Buddha is a form by which we can relate to truth."

"Is the Buddha an incarnation?"

"Oh, no. No. It is that to which we can relate in order to become free."

As we talked more about God, it was difficult for him. When I used the word, he pictured an old man with a heavy beard, who sat up in the sky. This he could not accept. He preferred to use the indefinite word "absolute."

"Buddhists do not believe in a personal God or Creator, but some believe that "mind" or "spirit" or "law" permeated all of space, and that all living things everywhere are part of it."

"Is there any concept of creation in Buddhism, or any beginning to life?"

"Not in that sense, no. No beginning and no end."

"Is there any explanation of the universe?"

"It is not made a problem," he said calmly. "What's the difference? We are here. We weren't there. Our problem is one of suffering. Whether the world was created or not, doesn't matter. The point is to achieve enlightenment in this life."

"What if you don't?"

"If you don't, then there is the wheel of life. You will come back in some other form."

"Who achieves this freedom? Will most devout Buddhists reach it?"

"I wouldn't say *most*. Not in this life, no."

"So there is enlightenment, as you put it, only after many lives."

He agreed. But he remained perfectly relaxed about it. I discovered that he believed in one hundred and eighty hells, from which everyone would eventually recover. A person could go down in the next life, regress instead of progress, but all will ultimately be saved. There were also thirty-three heavens through which one could move up.

"If it is true that all will reach enlightenment, then you don't have to convert anybody, do you?"

"No. And I get very uneasy when anybody tries to convert me."

I expected that answer. But I did ask: "Years ago Buddhism spread throughout Asia. Is there any missionary movement today?"

"I wouldn't call it a missionary movement then or now, although Buddhism did spread. But there is no missionary movement as such. We don't go out to get people. We talk to them if they come to us."

"Some Christians think that way, too." I couldn't help but interject that. It sounded like some churches I know.

But Christianity proceeds from a different base. I was coming to that now.

"What do you think of Jesus?" I asked John.

"Well." He signed. "I think of Him only as a good Jew. I don't think I can accept Him as part of the, what do you call it . . . ?"

"The Trinity?"

"Yes."

"Well, the Trinity is the result of our faith in Jesus. We do not begin there. And I don't really want to discuss it. What do you make of the teachings of Jesus? That's my question. Suppose Jesus said that He is the Son of God. What do you make of that?"

"Not being really too concerned about God, I don't make anything of it."

"But if a man came into the world and said, 'I came from (I will use your term) the "absolute," ' what would this convey to you?" I asked John eagerly.

"So is everyone else. But I would not use the term 'from.' I don't think that a term like that *could* be used. Certainly not by a Buddhist."

"That's exactly why I used it," I said. "This is what Christianity says to the world. This man came *from* God, *from* the Absolute, *from* the Infinite. Does this disturb you in any way?"

"It hasn't to date."

He was cautious.

"It has often been said," he now volunteered, "that Christianity is the religion of the "father" and Buddhism is the religion of the "mother." Where the father is stern and authoritarian, the mother is compassionate and loving."

"Would you rather have a mother-God?"

"A mother-God? That idea is also foreign to me. I don't know."

It was becoming obvious that God Himself was central to our discussion, and that unless he would begin to think of a Creator or Father or a God who loves man, we would get no further. The road was blocked.

"Let's talk about suffering then," I suggested. "Christianity has a cross at its center. That is basically a symbol of suffering."

"For us that seems a violent suffering. And this is not really the suffering we emphasize. We talk about torments bringing on neuroses and psychoses."

"But isn't death a part of suffering?"

"Sure. But it doesn't have much meaning. There are more important problems now," he said, still drawing readily on his pipe.

"You identify with those who suffer, don't you?"

"I try. Yet we are too egocentric to do much about it."

"We also talk about ego, pride and man's self-centeredness. We say that for this purpose Jesus died and gave His life. He sacrificed Himself in order that we might be forgiven."

"Hmmm. Put in those terms, I don't feel so antagonistic toward it. I might even be sympathetic."

"Suppose Christianity is true," I continued. "Would this mean anything to you? Suppose God came into man's world and willingly, voluntarily suffered on the cross? Does this convey anything to you about suffering? About God? About love? Let me put it this way. It seems to me that Buddhism attempts to escape from suffering, whereas Christianity declares that God actually walked into the pain of the cross—deliberately."

"This could be looked at as an act of achieving merit. The Buddha in many lives suffered before he became the Buddha."

"What if Jesus had already arrived?"

"In what sense?"

"Christianity speaks of only *one* life. Jesus is a unique person. He does not try to pile up favor with God. He *is* in a relationship with His Father, who is the Eternal God. Christianity says nothing about any previous lives."

He staggered about for a few moments. He could not respond. I concluded that I was speaking in a different language, and it had to take time to soak in. For those who think in totally diverse categories, the Christian faith falls at first on very hard ground.

"There is only one further step in the Christian

127

drama," I added. "What about Jesus' resurrection?"

"This is something beyond me. I've never given it any thought. It just doesn't sit with me."

"What if it happened? What if there was one Man who returned from the dead? What if . . . ?"

"What if it happened?" He repeated it, pulling comfort from his pipe. "I don't know. I can't conceive of an act like that."

"Neither can I," I said honestly.

"Well, my first reaction would be to test the fact with modern, scientific means. To prove it."

"Suppose it could be proven?"

"Well. I don't know. I might look upon it as a miracle. And this is the very reason why I won't accept it. We don't accept miracles."

As he sat there thinking, he kept on repeating to himself, "What if it happened? What if it really happened?"

After a long pause, he concluded: "I don't know. It's hard for me to answer this. It's simply out of my realm of thought. Even if such an event occurred, it would not be a proof of any other statements about Jesus, that He was the Son of God."

"But you would consider it unusual?"

"Obviously."

He stood to his feet and offered to show me around the temple. We took a short tour and exchanged pleasantries. As we shook hands to part, I couldn't help but sum up in my own mind what he had actually been saying.

Man is his own savior. He achieves enlightenment, eventually. He earns his own rewards, and they will bring him to heaven (nirvana). So man works his way to God. Grace does not really set him free.

Man's works mean that God is the object of our religious striving. God's grace means that we are the object of His love in action. The good news of God runs counter to all the ideologies of men.

CHAPTER 11

The (Hindu) Mystic

In the modern home of a modern intellectual, I talked with a man of great refinement. He had been brought up in the Hindu world of gods and disciplines, of endless cycles of cause and effect, birth and rebirth. But the extensive library on his shelves, the art objects and rich paintings which surrounded us, spoke of a person who had excellent taste, and who enjoyed the best of twentieth century culture.

His love of beauty and nature could be seen in his exotic garden, to which he devoted a lot of personal attention.

He was a quiet-spoken man, ready to denounce pride and arrogance, but obviously taking a keen interest in his own intellectual achievements. Nor could he camouflage his feelings of superiority over those who had not achieved as much as he, were not as educated as he, or belonged to what may be called the common people. He looked down on them as an adult looks

130

down on a child which isn't quite able to compete. As a mystic, he also looked down on organized religion, which ranged beneath him as little hills lie at the feet of a majestic mountain.

He was dressed comfortably. Knowing that I was a Christian, he opened the conversation by surprising me.

"Don't waste your time and energy on me," he said. "If you are going to talk about Jesus, I will tell you right away that I've always had the most profound respect and interest in Jesus. That may sound strange to you. I've had it almost from childhood. I was actually a Brahmin, from the highest caste in India, as you know. I'm not mentioning this snobbishly. . . ."

"I understand," I said. "But you take me by surprise. You have from early times thought about Jesus?"

"Almost intuitively," he replied. "I was steeped in the Vedas and ancient Hindu lore. I enjoyed listening to the musical language of the Vedas. But I had always that feeling. I don't know where I got it from. This was before I came to the West. And when I came to Cambridge, I studied medieval history. It was my special subject."

"Why did you choose Christian history?"

"I had an interest in it, that's all. Then I also studied law before graduating."

"Could you explain this feeling of reverence for Jesus? Would you say it is distinct from Buddha or anyone else?"

"I cannot say *distinct* from anyone else. Just as you love many people, so you don't love one as compared with someone else. I can't beat up a lot of explanations for it. Just, simple, direct—Jesus. But I feel so directly and intuitively for this, rather than for the Buddha or Shankara or Mohammed."

"Now, do you consider Jesus as one of the deities in Hinduism? There are many, of course. Do you think of Jesus as one of the great teachers, or a saint?"

"Deities don't appeal to me. Certain philosophical concepts of Krishna and Buddha, yes. I'm not an orthodox Hindu, or highly devoted to any of them, you see. I never was."

"My point is this." I tried to explain. "As you know, the Hindu mind can accept many teachers. The Jewish-Christian mind only accepts the one Messiah. Is it in this sense that you look at Jesus?"

"I'm not trying to give you explanations," he said, actually dodging the question a bit.

I still pursued. "A Hindu said to a Christian once that if an image of Christ is put into every Hindu temple, no Hindu will see the point of becoming a Christian."

"Why should everyone become a Christian?" he interrupted, shrugging his shoulders. "I have no interest in Christianity or the church as such. I'm opposed to the organization because it seems to distract me from the reality of Jesus. We should not be interested in the images created for us, the words spoken about Him, but in the actual being of Christ. It's like that saying that He comes like a thief in the night. Which means uninvited. I'm more interested in that coming of Christ to the heart, not in philosophical squabbles. When you see a rose, why do you demand a description from a botanist?"

"All right," I agreed. "But what does worship mean to you then?"

"Worship is love. What you love, you worship. As simple as that. And I feel that way about Christ. Explanations are unnecessary if the reality is there. Only those who are bereft like the desert demand explanations."

"I've heard that a Hindu can worship beneath an idol, walk a thousand miles to a holy river, take food to the monkeys or give alms to the poor, and all that is considered worship."

"Well, in a way, it is, isn't it? Whatever you do expresses your feelings."

He again spoke about Christ.

"I feel Him all the time, if I want to," he said. "Much of the time, I'm distracted, unfortunately."

"You came from a rigid upbringing in India. . . ."

"Oh, yes. The most rigid, orthodox group. You could compare it to the most orthodox of Jews or Christians. Those who adhere strictly to the letter of the law, you know. And I sometimes ask myself, why I am drawn to Christ. And I don't know why."

"Allow me to ask you how this relates to what you are living for?"

"You don't live *for* something. The constant problem of life is to be free, to be part of beauty and truth and love. Not to be encrusted by all kinds of worries and concepts. We came from God, we return to God. Of course, that shouldn't be interpreted in terms of nudism."

He didn't crack a smile.

"You don't mind if I'm a little facetious sometimes?" he asked.

"Not at all," I said. "I want you to be as honest and straightforward and facetious as you like."

It was clear what he was talking about. The things men experience cannot be put into words. To contain them in creeds also does violence. It's like the experience of beauty or truth or love, but to the mystic these are realities.

I now attempted to get to something more concrete.

"Most people have what may be called a message for the world. . . ."

"Do you think so?" he broke in. "Is that the way to put it? Does everyone have to have a message for the world? This means I have something to say to the world. I would put it differently. I would say, *my life* is the message. I don't have to talk about it, you see? I am a voice in the wilderness. Who listens?"

"Is this how we can solve the problems in the world—like war, for example?"

"Oh, that's different. You will never solve these problems by talking about love or truth or Christ. It is a subtle temptation to think that I can solve those problems anyway. I can only do that which is possible for one simple person."

He seemed to have withdrawn somewhat from society. Not like a rebel, but in an intellectual atmosphere, a circle of experience which included him and a few who thought alike.

Now he talked about the ego, man's pride. It was really arrogance to think man can solve the problems of the world.

"What can we do about this ego?" I asked.

"You can't do anything about me," he replied quickly. "You can only do something about yourself. I about myself. That's a big enough job, isn't it?"

"To what extent does the Christian teaching of

forgiveness enter into this? Or, let me put it this way, does the death of Jesus have any meaning for you?"

"Well, I'll tell you something. There came to me a feeling yesterday. It came from the Last Supper. You know, Jesus said, 'This is My body.' For the first time I had the most extraordinary experience, a feeling of sacrifice, the giving of life for another. It was a feeling rather than a thought that this had been given. That's the best I can do with words. I was shocked by this feeling, wonderfully shocked, happily shocked. And that, to me, is life. That is the truth. 'I die that you may live.' That is love. I've never experienced anything like this before. Perhaps," he paused, "Perhaps it was a sign before your coming today."

He reflected on the thought again.

"These are the moments that re-create me. For someone who has wandered away, these are the moments that bring me back."

"I realize that I'm destroying it by talking with you about it," I proposed.

"No, you don't destroy it. You firm it in my mind. Nor can you take it away. It's there. And unless I gloat over the experience, it can't be destroyed."

His wife entered to serve us some tea. She was light skinned with long, flowing black hair and quite some years younger than he. She was very efficient about it and having served us, excused herself almost immediately again.

"May I ask you another question about Jesus? What of the resurrection? What do you make of this?"

"I don't want to get into it theologically." He stopped to drink some tea. "You see, to me, there is no death at all. It is a transformation if you want to call it that, from one state to another. For such immortals as Jesus, there is no death. God doesn't die. And Christ is God, not only the Son of God. So, in one way, there is no resurrection either."

"I'm trying to understand you."

"It's hard to explain," he continued. "It's not a concept of mine, or a theory, clearing away the verbal misconceptions. Simply—there is no death."

"Philosophically?"

"No, actually. Tomorrow I may be run over, of course. Or you. I don't mean it like that. Life is reality. The constant movement of life is life. *We* are life. So, there is no death."

"Do you see any parallel in this death and resurrection of Christianity to any other religion?"

"As a concept, no. Not at all. Not in Hinduism or Buddhism. There is immortality, of course."

"I was interested in this since you are a student of all religions," I said. "But what happens to us when we get run over, as you said?"

"Our bodies die, certainly. But you and I are part of life. Life goes on in spite of the body."

"Did Jesus die and rise bodily?"

"Oh, no. Nothing physical. Don't come with theories and theologies. Come only at the truth of life itself. This is what I have always felt. This is what I told you about when we first began to talk. I have felt so serene since those words 'this is My body' came to me."

"I would interpret that as Jesus giving Himself for us."

"Yes."

"And, since you said that Jesus is God, this God

136

gives Himself for us, mere humans."

"Oh, don't say *mere* humans," he broke in. "We are God, too. There is neither arrogance nor humility in this statement. God isn't humble or arrogant. He just *is*. This is the true state of balance. Of course, if I'm consciously arrogant, I try to appear humble. These are the tricks of the mind which we have taught ourselves, to appear different."

"It was Gandhi who said that if Jesus were God Himself, all men could be God Himself."

"Of course," he agreed. "This is what I'm trying to say. We are God, too. That is the phenomenon."

"I would say that we are created in the image of God, but that's not the same thing at all. Christians affirm that Jesus was God, but He alone. But allow me to ask you a related question," I continued. "How do you interpret the grace of God?"

"The grace of God is there all the time. We reject it by enclosing ourselves within ourselves, and then we say to ourselves, 'I'm happy. I'm wonderful.' We build walls. The grace of God is not something you have to beg for. It is the immediate, lasting, permanent destruction of the self. All this is symbolically dramatized in the story of Christ."

"Was there a death for the body of Christ?"

"Probably. All created things die. Ashes to ashes. . . ."

"Then resurrection is not related to the body?"

"No, it cannot be. That is a crude form of belief, the raising up of skeletons and all that. It's all a muddying up, a deterioration of pure reality."

And then quite suddenly it was all over. He stood up and thanked me for coming, and invited me to return.

137

"Not to theologize to you, or you to me. Just to talk."

It was not possible to speak any more about the good news of God. He had made up his mind. He had positioned himself above the mundane interpretations of the church. There seems to be no possible meeting between such people and the established church. But then, there never has been, in the formal sense.

And yet I came away from the conversation with a feeling of assurance. God reaches into many lives. In His own way. This Hindu valued his experience. It was genuine. And he related it to Christ, the light which lights *every* man who comes into the world!

I could not help but make a comparison. I thought of the glib Christian, the man who swallows it all hook, line and sinker, but never gives much thought to Christ. Who really feels the presence of God? Who really lives out the meaning of faith? Who will fare better at the judgment?

CHAPTER 12
The Christian Scientist

High up in the hills overlooking the sparkling city, a handsome man, greying at the temples, invited me into his luxurious home. It was a tastefully furnished house with a touch of early American, even a New England look. Through a large picture window I saw an inviting swimming pool, lit with underwater lighting, from which warm vapors rose in the cool of the night.

In the spacious living room Art sat down in a reclining chair with his feel up on a hassock. Joan, his wife, entered, comfortably attired in evening slacks, and immediately slipped to the floor where she seemed to feel more at ease.

The combination of early American furniture inside

and the relaxed atmostphere at the pool outside, was more than a meeting of East and West. It reflected the interests of two people and harmonized with their faith and outlook on life.

"As a Christian Scientist we believe that there is no such thing as sickness," Art started off. "I know that sounds strange to you. But, you see, I even get disturbed when I hear an aspirin commercial."

"Have you ever taken any aspirin?" I asked.

"Never." They both shook their heads.

"What's wrong with it?"

"Well, I've been raised in Science from infancy," said Joan. "I grew up with the idea that I was God's perfect child. Since I was God's perfect child, I was not capable of experiencing any kind of illness, anything that was alien to God's perfect nature."

"Did you ever get sick?"

"Yes. I went through all those childhood diseases."

"And then?"

"My mother and father called the practitioner. He would offer a silent or prayer treatment. He made certain declarations to my parents, that since I was God's perfect child and incapable of. . . ."

"I don't understand," I broke in. "How can you reconcile being God's perfect child with illness?"

"Illness is a lie. It is not the good. We trace *all* sickness to fear and mental causes. So we are not really sick. We only think we are. It's a belief. We have to get rid of that belief. It's the power of positive thinking, if you like. There is no sickness. All is 'infinite mind.' And in due time I'd get over it."

"Without any medication?"

"Exactly."

"What would happen to you if you could not lean on Christian Science?"

"I don't know."

"Would you consider going to a doctor?"

"I would be afraid to," volunteered Art. "I would not be able to trust him. I have no faith that I can be healed, except through Science."

"One time my mother had a sore on her face," said Joan. She wasn't the world's best Christian Scientist, although she liked to think so. The sore wouldn't heal. She became frightened. It lingered for months, and, of course, she feared a malignancy. Finally she went to a doctor, because she wasn't getting healed. She had an operation, and it turned out all right."

Art jumped in again. "If the conditions are met in Science there is *always* healing. If there is no healing, the conditions have not been met."

"If sickness is an illusion, what about death?"

"Call it passing on," said Art. "Death is a lie. We deny death. You see, we don't really exist. We're not real. It's like looking in a mirror. What you see is your reflection, not you. We are reflections of God. That's what we are. We are made in the image of God and reflect Him. So, when we pass on, it's like turning out the light. Then you can't look in the mirror any more. Then you go back to God."

"You say we're not real, but only reflections," I continued. "Didn't something happen to us, to man? Haven't we defected from that image of God?"

"No. Take the biblical story of the fall of man, to which you probably have reference."

"All right."

"It's only a means of depicting an illusion. It's an

141

allegory. It never really happened to the real man, to our true nature, to the pure and innocent image of God. Sin never touched the real self, the man of God's creating. We are without spot, without guilt, without blame."

"God's perfect children," said Joan.

"The thinking of mankind has been saturated for thousands of years with a sense of guilt," continued Art. "But the teachings of Christ, as interpreted by Mary Baker Eddy, liberate us from all that. Man is pure and innocent, made in the likeness of God."

"What do you think of God?"

"We worship God. We love God. He is the underlying premise of all life. God is in and through all creation and nature. God is all in all. God is love, love is God. God is spirit, spirit is God. God is soul, soul is God. God is both father and mother. Since God created man male and female, woman is left out, if God is merely a father. That is not to say that God is a person in the ordinary sense of the word. He is intelligence, infinite mind."

"Let's talk about Jesus," I said.

"All right," said Art. "He was a good man. A master. The herald of Christ-truth. You see, Jesus was the name of a man who presented Christ, the true idea of God, the spirit of truth and love. We see a dual nature. To us the Christ-spirit is the important thing. Jesus is not as important to us as He is to you."

"What do you think of the death of Jesus? Was it real?"

"If you're talking about a substitutionary death, we don't think that Jesus endured the cross in order to appease an angry God. The blood of Jesus cannot

142

cleanse from sin in death, any more than it could when it flowed in His veins. Rather, by His suffering He shows us the nature of God as love, and the way *we* can overcome pain and death."

"I don't believe that Jesus appeased an *angry* God either," I countered. "But I believe the Bible, when it says that He died for our sins. Is it superfluous to ask about Jesus' resurrection?"

It was. Since sin is unreal, and death an illusion, there would be no need for a resurrection.

"The deathless Christ-spirit ever lives," Art answered. "The material concept, or Jesus, simply disappeared. Mind is fundamental, not matter. Only by accepting the spiritual and not the physical, can we come to the truth."

I could not let it go so easily.

"What of the Bible itself?" I pressed. "It states that Jesus died for our sins! If you believe the Bible. . . ."

"I can't accept that," answered Joan now. "I am God's perfect child. Sin is a belief. It is unreal. We are incapable of sin. We cannot sin."

"Do you believe the Bible is the Word of God?"

"Yes."

"Then what do you make of this summation by the apostle Paul: 'All have sinned and come short of the glory of God'?" (Romans 3:23, K.J.V.).

"We aren't great Bible students," they said candidly. "But there is no disharmony between what we believe and the Bible. Mary Baker Eddy's ideas are all from the Bible. She interprets it for us. Her book throws light on the Bible and unlocks scientific truth and principles. She explains the Bible to us."

"If Christianity has been preaching for centuries that

143

Jesus came to take away our sins, and if man is a sinner who needs redemption, how can this harmonize with your teaching?"

Joan rose quietly and poured some coffee she had prepared. She brought back a couple of pieces of cake, topped with whipped cream. For Art and me. I asked her why she wasn't having any. She was on a diet. We sipped our coffee.

"I know that sin and salvation aren't necessarily pleasant words to your ears," I said. "But you have allowed me to talk with you, and you can see that you have a very different interpretation of the Bible."

"Yes," she said. "That's it. It's all in your interpretation."

Art was busy eating his cake, but Joan was beginning to wrestle with it in her mind.

"I have been taught that I am spiritual and perfect, the reflection of eternal mind." She was thinking out loud. "If I were to accept that I am a sinner, then I would need a Saviour. And, of course, the Bible would mean all that literally. I would have to accept all this about salvation. . . ."

I let her talk on.

"I don't know," she mused. "I just don't know. But I've always been interested in the Bible."

"Do you think that God would lie?"

"Of course not." It shocked her.

"Then, the Scriptures are true?"

"Yes. But I believe that Mary Baker Eddy gives us an authoritative interpretation."

"She is an honest person?"

"Yes."

"But if she says one thing and the Bible teaches

something else, to what conclusion do you come?"

"I don't know."

"And God cannot lie!" I quoted from I John 1:10: "If we say we have committed no sin, we make him out to be a liar."

"Is that in the Bible?"

"Yes. And the passage goes on to say: 'And then his word has no place in us.'"

"I can't draw any conclusions yet. . . ."

"Of course," I said gently. "All I can hope is that you examine the Bible for yourself. Find out what it really says."

"I'm willing," she replied. Art still busied himself with his cake. "Remember though, I have been brought up in Science since childhood. It's never occurred to me that I was a sinner and needed a Saviour. As other Christians say."

"Think about the history of Christianity. Think about all the people who lived before Mary Baker Eddy brought her teaching into the world."

"That's right. But the idea of Christian Science always existed in the bosom of God. It needed her to come along and reveal it."

"But what of the wisdom of Augustine, the faith of Luther, the revival under Wesley? Are they all insignificant? Less important than she?"

"I've never thought about that too much. No, they weren't unimportant. But it was not the light of science and health, which reveal the unreality of sin and disease and. . . ."

Her voice trailed off.

They were really two very intelligent people tied, like their furniture, to aristocratic Boston in a relaxed atmosphere of their heated swimming pool.

Now Art finished his whipped cream topping. "Everyone is good," he said. "Evil is nonexistent. The belief in sin must be abolished. Man should realize what he is. There is no death. There is no hell. Heaven fills all. The Christ-spirit ever lives. God is all in all."

It was coming out like information that had been fed into a computer, without errors—his version. And along with it a tolerance of what others believe, a permissiveness. After all, it was not a life or death, heaven or hell issue.

I now tried another avenue.

"Have you ever heard that Mary Baker Eddy is supposed to have worn glasses and false teeth?"

"I don't believe it." They both cried out. "That isn't true."

"Did you know she is supposed to have used drugs on occasion?"

"Who would tell such lies? Where did you hear this? Someone is being unkind!"

"What if I showed you a picture of her wearing glasses?"

"It would be a touched-up photograph!"

"All right. Let me go along with you. Suppose these are all lies. I did not bring up the subject to be unkind or vindictive. I want to make quite *another* point. Don't you agree that such insinuations (if they are not true) are wrong, evil, unkind as you say?"

"Of course."

"Then, how can you affirm there is no evil in the world? No sin in man? How is it possible to say that we are all God's perfect children, when these 'children' viciously attack and hate?"

We sat quietly for a moment. They let it sink in.

"It's not real," said Art.

"Isn't this attack on Mary Baker Eddy real?"

They were a little uncomfortable. Joan switched the subject.

"You know, we were away from Science for awhile. Nothing was happening in our family. We had job failures. Financial pressures. The children were always sick. It was a rough period. We didn't go to church at all."

"I was in the kind of work," said Art, "that when you finished a job, you were out of work. Nothing would last. It was pretty rough going."

"That's when I suggested we'd better go back to Christian Science, and work at it." Joan sounded firm as she recalled the past.

It was hard to believe in this spacious, comfortable home that they had ever seen difficult times. And now, in spite of an upturn in the economy, they attributed their financial success to Science.

"We were receptive and found peace of mind. The Christ-truth came through to us."

"But now what you're talking about," began Art again. "It's all in the way you look at it. It's not that we say there is no sin. It's just that we say it's *unreal*. It doesn't exist. We don't make God a liar. It's not possible. We have another interpretation, a spiritual interpretation. And you don't."

Joan wasn't swayed. In fact, she turned to Art now: "When we say it's unreal and doesn't exist, we're actually saying there is no sin or death. But the Bible doesn't put it like that. I can't dismiss that verse about making God a liar so lightly. I wish I could. But I'm going to have to think about it some more."

She stood to her feet to take out the empty dishes. "Will you come back so we can talk again?" It was a gracious invitation from a lady who knew how to entertain graciously. She meant it.

We said good-night and I thanked them both for the evening. They were most kind.

As I drove down the hill, I felt that if Joan was beginning to question the Bible, she would be receptive to its message. After all, what Jesus asks of us, at the start, is to learn from Him.

SUMMARY

The Tolerant

It is as difficult to speak to a person who wishes to include Jesus as one of the great teachers of the world, as it is to one who dismisses Him in favor of some other authority. Only it requires a different approach. This inclusive view negates the uniqueness of the person of Jesus, and presses the words of Jesus into a mold for which they were never intended. And it's simply unfair to force an interpretation on the Bible which is foreign to its intent. (Of course, that's sometimes happened inside Christianity, too.)

The Buddhist must first of all come to grips with the fact of God. God, the Creator, the one who says "I am." How can the unique entry of God into human flesh hold any meaning without such a prior belief in God? So, with Buddhists we may have to start at the very foundation.

The Hindu looks at Christianity through the colored glasses of his Eastern views. He can't see Christ as the Messiah—for all men. If only he could remove those glasses and accept the Christian revelation as the **Christian** revelation. He may then realize that one cannot squeeze the Bible through his own sieve of interpretation.

The Christian Scientist has a more particular problem. We must not only challenge the views of Mary Baker Eddy. We need to present the words of Jesus in the context in which they appear. The Scientist must face the reality of sin and death, and think through the meaning of the cross and resurrection.

It could very well be said that the tolerant, permissive person, as well as the militant, is working his way to God (if he believes in God). Religion, apart from Christianity, generally becomes a do-it-yourself program. But that's not good news.

When man has to save himself by his own efforts, he does not freely enter into the grace of God. If it is by works it is no longer of grace. This is the choice Christianity always presents over against the religious views of men.

CHAPTER 13

A Final Observation

If there is one lesson I have learned from these conversations with people of other beliefs, it's that there is no *one* way to "convert the world." Not only are the religious expressions of man diverse, but so are people within the religions. There can never be one formula, one set of laws, nor any stereotyped pattern used to preach Christianity.

It would be so much simpler if there could. But that's an empty dream.

Even Jesus didn't proceed in this way. He didn't walk about saying the same things in the same words to everybody. Only *once* did He tell a man that he had to be born again. And never during His ministry did He give His disciples a system of beliefs, a creedal statement to propound, or a set method by which they were to "win souls."

It's far more complex.

First, I think, we must find out where a person stands, what he really believes. Is he a realist or an escapist? Is he exclusive or tolerant? That's important. Not that you want to compartmentalize people, but you must have some idea of their position. Or else you're shooting in the dark. Sometimes you may hit the target that way, but generally it's sheer luck.

Jesus listened to people before he made any attempt to speak to their condition. Even so, some accepted what He had to say; others refused Him. That means Jesus did not enjoy one hundred percent success. If we really believe this, it will free us from the compulsion to succeed.

Let no one get the impression, however, that sharing the good news is a discouraging business. You may have thought so after reading this book, or from your own experiences. It isn't. If Jesus thought it worth His while to suffer with us and for us, and then wanted to send us into all the world to tell the story of his coming, His death and resurrection, who are we to despair of the enterprise?

There is always a temptation to give up after you have failed. Failure has a way of dampening the spirit. Again, consider Jesus. He experienced failure after failure with many who heard Him, rejection from the religious community which worshiped God, expulsion from villages that had other pursuits, misunderstanding from His family and friends. Nevertheless, He refused to give in to discouragement. He set His face straight for the storm in Jerusalem. The cross itself looked like utter failure, but it became the door to triumph and a mission into all the world.

Besides. We don't "convert" anybody. God does. His

Spirit is at work in His world, and, I've discovered, sometimes quite apart from us. We believe in Him who has taken the initiative and entered the world for our salvation. This faith should free us from the pressure some Christians feel, a pressure induced by a certain type of preaching, which makes witnessing a duty instead of a joy. But if we are tense when we confront a person of another faith or no faith, we can hardly be free to become instruments of the Spirit of God.

There is no pat formula. Paul emphasized this when he said that he became all things to all men, that by all means he would win some. The Jew he approached as a Jew, the Greek as a Greek. He did not drive home the meaning of the Ten Commandments to people who had not heard them.

Do you realize that leaves the field wide open for us?

Only he who listens to another has the right to speak to him. And, only he who listens will know what to say! Besides, at times we ought to give a cup of cold water in the name of Christ, before we can even say a word to another person.

Let us be receptive to God. Let us grow in the grace and knowledge of Jesus Christ. Let us be guided by the Spirit, and the desire to share the good news will arise within us.

It is good news for *every* person, no matter what his religious or nonreligious beliefs. Jesus sends us into all the world—the world He loves, and for which He gave His life.